THE LIFE OF GRACE

Teacher's Manual

Faith and Life Series

BOOK SEVEN

Ignatius Press, San Francisco
Catholics United for the Faith, New Rochelle

Nihil Obstat: Msgr. Michael J. Wrenn, M.A., M.S.
                  Censor Librorum
Imprimatur: + Joseph T. O'Keefe, D.D.
                  Vicar General, New York

Director: Rev. Msgr. Eugene Kevane, Ph.D.
Assistant Director and General Editor: Patricia I. Puccetti, M.A.
Writer: Sister Mary Catherine Blanding, I.H.M.

Catholics United for the Faith, Inc., and Ignatius Press gratefully acknowledge the guidance and assistance of
Reverend Monsignor Eugene Kevane, former Director of the Pontifical Catechetical Institute, Diocese of
Arlington, Virginia, in the production of this series. The series intends to implement the authentic approach in
Catholic catechesis given to the Church in the recent documents of the Holy See and in particular the Conference
of Joseph Cardinal Ratzinger on "Sources and Transmission of Faith".

CONTENTS

APPENDIX

Introduction

Principles

TEXT AND GRADE LEVEL

The text for the seventh grade is devoted to the life of grace, that real life with which Mother Church nurtures us in the sacraments, and on which all Catholic life is centered. As a preparation, the first six chapters deal with natural and supernatural revelation, and lead up to the mission of Christ and his Church. Seventh-graders, facing the onset of puberty, can be idealistic and open to the gift of grace; at this age they are able to reason and abstract more, so the text brings out more the specific role of reason in their lives as Catholics.

CATECHESIS: NATURE AND PURPOSE

Because of your willingness to share your time and talent, you have entered more fully into one of the Church's most important and sacred duties, that of making Christ better known and loved by his children, young or old. This duty of the Church entails handing on the message of God, in its entirety and purity. You cannot mix God's message with political or social views without betraying the Divine mission. Political and social trends come and go, but the word of God is always timely. Catechesis must be based on Revelation as transmitted by the universal Teaching Authority of the Church, in its solemn or ordinary form (CT 52, cf. *Dei Filius* chapter 3). The doctrine you hand on by your teaching is received by your students as it truly is, the very Word of God, accepted as it is taught, namely, on the authority of God revealing (cf. 1 Th 2:13). This teacher's manual is designed to help you in this important work of handing on the living and unchanging Word of God.

Catechetics, according to the *General Catechetical Directory,* is the form of the ministry of the word of God, "which is intended to make men's faith become living, conscious, and active, through the light of instruction" (GCD 17). This instruction presupposes that the student already knows and believes in at least the basics of the gospel as taught by the Church. A good way to determine the depth of your students' knowledge of the faith is to ask them the basic questions listed in the Appendix. It will then be easier to know which students require more fundamental instruction.

THE CATECHIST: CHRIST'S INSTRUMENT

If teaching religion seems like a big task, that is only because it *is* a big task! But don't get worried! As Pope John Paul II said in *Catechesi Tradendae:* "It is Christ . . . who is taught . . . and it is Christ alone who teaches" (CT 6). This statement means that you are Christ's instrument; through you he will spread his message. You have a very important role in faithfully passing on the message of the gospel, the constant, unchanging message: Jesus Christ, the only begotten Son of God, made man. On the other hand, you also have the assurance that God is going to help you every step of the way in proclaiming his message. You, too, have the guarantee given to the apostles: "I will be with you always even to the end of the world" (cf. Mt 28:20).

You are also very important because it is the living catechist, the living example, who gets the message across. No matter which text you use, no matter which method you choose, it will be the message you present, your living of the gospel, your likeness to Christ that will be most important in bringing your students closer to Christ (cf. GCD 71). Consequently, you need to prepare yourself for the task, always confident that if you do your part God will do his. The best way to prepare yourself is to pray, to study, to pray, to plan, and to pray.

THE ROLE OF THE PARENTS: THE FIRST CATECHISTS

The family provides the first and irreplaceable introduction to Christian faith and practice for any child. Parents are the first instructors of their children. The instruction in the faith, which starts from the earliest age, should include not only the parents' good Christian example, but also a formation in prayer and an explanation and review of what their children have learned about the faith from methodical religious instruction and liturgical events (CT 68). (In some situations where the children attend neither a Catholic school nor a CCD class because these are not available or are inadequate, the parents [or the grandparents] are the *only* source of catechetical instruction. If this situation is yours, God bless your efforts and may this series help you in the children's formation in Christ.)

Parent cooperation is very important to a teacher's success as a catechist. You should try to involve parents in their children's instruction: sharing with them the program and methods you are using, consulting them about better ways to reach their children or to help with problems that may arise. Let the parents know that you are there to help them fulfill their duties in forming and educating their children in Christ (cf. GCD 78, 79).

Practicalities

LESSON PLANNING

Lesson planning is very important for an organized and successful teacher. It helps you cover all the material systematically in the time that you have available.

The first step in planning is to make an overview of everything you want to teach during the year. For example, there are thirty chapters in the seventh grade text, but suppose you are in a CCD program and you are going to have only twenty-eight classes during the school year. You will need to plan which lessons you can combine and which lessons you might want to expand over two or three weeks. If you have the students every weekday, the overview is also helpful to you in scheduling what needs to be covered every week so that nothing is left out or covered too quickly. Included in the Appendix is a chart to help you plan your course for the year.

The second step is to plan the daily lesson so as to reach the students on as many levels as possible. The *General Catechetical Directory* #70 mentions *experience, imagination, memory,* and *intelligence* as different faculties of the children that should be active in the task of learning. A good lesson plan will involve all of these faculties.

RECOMMENDED CATECHETICAL SOURCES

Catechism of Christian Doctrine, published by order of Pope St. Pius X, trans. Rev. Msgr. Eugene Kevane (Arlington, Va., Center for Family Catechetics, 1980). (The questions in the children's texts are from this catechism.)

Hardon, John A., S.J., *The Catholic Catechism* (New York: Doubleday and Co., Inc., 1975), 623 pages.

Lawler, Ronald, O.F.M., Cap., Donald W. Wuerl, and Thomas Comerford Lawler, editors, *The Teaching of Christ: A Catholic Catechism for Adults,* 2nd ed. (Huntington: Our Sunday Visitor, Inc., 1983), 640 pages.

The Roman Catechism, translated and annotated by Rev. Robert I. Bradley, S.J. and Rev. Msgr. Eugene Kevane (Boston: St. Paul Editions, 1985), 586 pages.

Sharing the Light of Faith, National Conference of Catholic Bishops (Washington, D.C.: United States Catholic Conference, 1979).

Vatican Council II: The Conciliar and Post Conciliar Documents, gen. ed. Austin Flannery, O.P. (New York: Costello Publishing, 1975).

Vatican Council II, More Post Conciliar Documents, gen. ed. Austin Flannery, O.P. (New York: Costello Publishing, 1982). (This volume includes *Catechesi Tradendae,* and the *General Catechetical Directory,* both vital documents for the Catechist.)

POINTS ON TEACHING CHILDREN

1. The first thing necessary for successfully communicating the message of the

gospel is to have a genuine love for the gospel and for your students; all else flows from this love. A genuine love consists of desiring the greatest good for your students, which necessitates maintaining a fair and consistent discipline. Your task is not merely to teach a subject matter but to form children in the image of Christ. State clearly your requirements and the reasons behind them. Do not let the rules slip. If you have made something a policy stick to it! Jesus himself was gentle but firm.

2. Learn the names of your students as quickly as possible. This small effort will help you maintain discipline and let your students know that you care enough about them to remember who they are.

3. Try to call on everyone, not just on those students who volunteer: in this way everyone remains attentive and the shy students have an opportunity to come out of themselves.

4. Give clear directions for assignments. For example, do the first part of the assignment with the children or do the assignments or activities yourself beforehand so that you are familiar with the problems your students might have. Walk around the classroom so that you can give individual attention to those students having difficulties.

5. If you notice a normally attentive student not paying attention, find out what the problem is and be willing to take the time (outside of class time if possible) to help or find someone who can.

6. When using the chalkboard, remember to start at the left-hand side. Skipping around is extremely confusing for the students.

7. Overplan. It is all right if you run out of time; it can be a disaster if you run out of material to teach.

8. Review the lesson with your students at the end of the class period and review the lesson again at the beginning of the next class before starting the new lesson. Repetition *is* the mother of learning.

Suggested Introductory Lesson

Aims:

To find out how much the students know and understand about their faith; to get to know the students and to familiarize them with class content and procedure.

Materials Needed:

Student texts and activity books, folders with students' names on them (optional), name tags (optional), seating chart (optional), game or quiz (see the Appendix for game), paper and pencils.

Procedure

1. Pray.

2. Play a name game to learn your students' names, or give them name tags, or make a seating chart beforehand.

3. Hand out text and activity books. (You might supply your students with folders in which to keep books, papers and pencils.)

4. Ask the basic catechism questions from the Appendix, either in the form of a quiz or a game.

5. Introduce the subject the students will be studying during the year.

6. Assign the students Chapter 1 of the textbook to read. (You might find it more practical to have the reading assignment read and discussed during the class covering the particular chapter rather than assign it as homework).

7. Pray.

PART ONE

God
Reveals Himself

CHAPTER 1

Knowing God Through Creation

Background Reading for the Teacher:

Lawler, pp. 29–42, 47–52, 56–58 (second edition).
Hardon, pp. 34–41, 53–67.

Aims:

The students should be able to explain a natural knowledge of God's existence through order and design; to identify man as a composition of body and soul and explain the difference between humans and animals; to perceive the role of faith and reason; to understand the role of revelation in making knowledge of God more perfect; and to identify the attributes of God.

Materials Needed:

Paper, pen or pencil, chalkboard, Bibles, magazines with pictures of nature (optional), letters of the alphabet cut up (optional), light bulbs of differing colors (optional).

Activities

1. Write on the board in large capital letters GOD, so the students will see the topic for the week. Ask leading questions. "Did you ever wonder whether God really exists? Did you ever meet someone who did not believe in God? How do we really know God exists?" Explain how important, above all other truths, is the existence of God. Compare his existence to any other basic truth. "You must learn the letters of the alphabet before reading; you must learn arithmetic before learning algebra. (You cannot do complicated division problems if you do not know that $2 + 2 = 4$!)"

"God's existence can be compared to a light bulb." (Here you might want to hold up light bulbs of differing colors. "If I put a purple light bulb in this room, so that we have nothing but purple lights, what color would the room be? If

I put a green . . ." (Go on.) "You see, the light bulb influences the way I see everything else. So my belief in God and my knowledge of who he is influences the way I see everybody and everything."

2. "Are Christians and Jews the only ones who believe in God?" Tell the students about ancient cultures that built temples and offered sacrifices to gods. Show them pictures from *National Geographic* or other sources of temples, tombs, altars, and so on. The Greek and Roman gods are very interesting. Make the point that all peoples of all times have believed in a god or gods.

3. Direct your students to open their Bibles to Rom 1:20. Ask someone to read. Ask, "What does St. Paul mean?" Make up a chart or compose a meditation on "Scripture References on God's Existence" (such as Rom 1:20; Wis 11:15; 13:1–9; Acts 17:24–29; 1 Cor 1:21; 49:26–28; Ps 106:20; 14:1; 53:1; Is 2:6; 5:21).

4. Point out the absurdity of the argument for chance. Describe or actually place letters of the alphabet (cut out from cardboard) in a large container. Shake the container and let the letters fall. Explain that having the universe come about by chance is like having a book come about by an author "shaking" the letters about. Ask the students what they think.

5. Ask the students to think of one thing that reminds them of God. Or bring out magazines and tell them to look for anything in nature that points to God's existence. Collect fascinating truths of nature, which show clearly God's planning (for example, some insects have eight hundred legs, etc.).

6. Remind your students of the need for example in converting others from atheism. Tell the story of St. Vincent de Paul and the galley slaves. "St. Vincent de Paul lived in France at a time when prisoners were condemned to be galley slaves. A galley slave would spend his entire day rowing ships where he would be chained. It would be very hot and uncomfortable and he was usually treated very harshly. St. Vincent knew how much Jesus loved these men, and even though they cursed God and acted as if God did not exist, St. Vincent—a priest, and a very busy one at that—would go up to these men, kiss their hands, and ask with the greatest courtesy if he could help them. He himself would row with them. He never spoke about God, yet his example converted many from atheism. This shows how example is important in winning others to God." Have the students write a monologue describing how a saint converted atheists by his example alone.

7. Show, by chalk talk A, how man is composed of body and soul. Draw on the board a stick figure of a man. "Man has a body. How do we know?" "Man has a soul. How do we know?"

8. Pretend to your students you do not believe in a soul. If they cannot point out your errors, give them this simple argument: "Do you think? Can you see your thinking? Well, if you do not believe in a soul because you cannot see it, then I do not believe in your thinking, because I do not see it!"

9. Make a chart on the board, or direct your students to make one, showing the differences between animals and humans. Ask them the names of their pets. Ask, "Can Fido pray to God? Does Fido think about heaven? Does

18

Chalk Talk Ⓐ

Man is like a bridge

Material World   Spiritual World

Body   Soul

Man / Animals / Plants / Inanimate creation (rocks, water, etc.)

Highest of the visible (why?)

Lowest of the spiritual (why?)

God / Angels / Man

Fido think? Can Fido read? Can Fido plan a party? Can Fido control his instincts? Can Fido come to our religion class, sit in a desk, and raise his paw, as you can?" Point out that, although animals have affections and emotions, they do not have human affections and human emotions.

10. Do activity no. III on p. 7 in the Activity Book.

11. Ask the students, "What is faith? Is faith the same as reason? Do they contradict each other?" See chalk talk B.

12. Direct the students to read in class references associated with God's attributes that show he is:
    All-present (Wis 1:7; Ps 139:8–10);
    All-knowing (Ps 90:2–4; 130:1–2; Rev 1:8; Mt 6:8; 10:36;
    All-powerful (Wis 11:25; Mt 19:26; Gen 17:1; 43:14; Lk 1:37);

All-merciful (Ex 34:6–7; Mt. 9:13; 1 Jn 3:16).

Here are some questions and comments on the attributes of God to be asked during or after the Bible reading.

All-present:
"God is everywhere. What does this mean? Is he in our classroom right now? What does it mean to walk in the presence of God? Just think: God is here right now in our room. How good we should be knowing God is here. It is like having a priest, a parent, or a teacher" (mention someone they all know and respect) "with you at a party. How good you would be! Let us try to keep in the presence of God."

All-knowing:
"God knows everything . . . even our most secret thoughts and desires. If he knows everything, everything should be worthy of his knowledge. If he

19

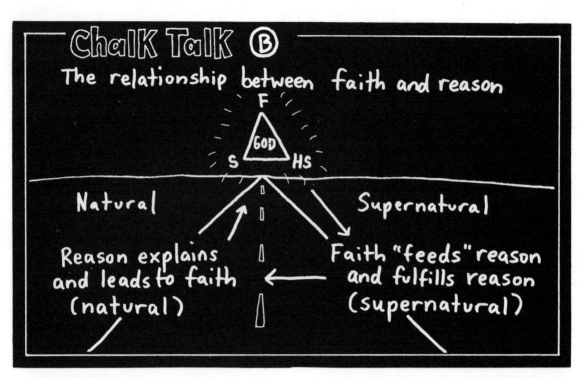

Chalk Talk B

The relationship between faith and reason

F
GOD
S   HS

Natural   Supernatural

Reason explains   Faith "feeds" reason
and leads to faith   and fulfills reason
(natural)   (supernatural)

---

knows everything, he also understands our problems, and we should talk to him about them."

All-powerful:
"Have you ever been in a jet airplane? Have you ever been in the ocean, caught by a wave? Have you ever seen the redwoods or ever been to Yellowstone National Park? Have you ever seen the Grand Canyon? All these things remind us of God's power. Remember, he is all-powerful and can do anything; he holds us in his hand right now and keeps you and me alive."

All-merciful:
"St. Thérèse is a famous teenage saint. When she was just a little older than you, she discovered the deepness of God's mercy and was so excited. God is always ready to forgive us, if we are sorry for offending him. Let us trust in his mercy."

13. To present a lesson on the Trinity, tell the story of St. Augustine. "One day St. Augustine was sitting on a beach. He looked very sad. Suddenly, a little boy asked why he was so sad. 'I cannot understand the Trinity', said St. Augustine. The little boy began digging a hole in the sand. 'Do you see this hole?' 'Yes.' 'Do you see that ocean?' 'Yes.' 'Trying to fill this hole with all the drops of the ocean is like trying to understand the Trinity.' With that, the little boy disappeared, and St. Augustine realized now how foolish his sadness had been."

14. Give the students the following role-play instructions:
    a. "Pretend you are a missionary and want to tell others about the Trinity. We will pretend to be pagans. Prepare a speech or give some examples that might help convert us."

b. "Prepare a 'lesson' for first-graders on the Trinity. You will be the teacher, and all the others will be first-graders." (Let them act like first-graders for this; it adds to the fun.)

Lesson Plan for a One-day Presentation

1. Pray the Glory Be.

2. See activities 1–14, above.

3. Assign p. 7 in the Activity Book.

Suggested Schedule for a Five-day Presentation

1. The existence of God
   Aim: to identify God's existence through order, design, and the wonders of nature; to perceive the importance of God's existence; and to perceive how all peoples of all times have seen that God does exist.
   Activities: see activities 1, 2, 3, 4, 5, and 6.

2. The existence of God
   Aim: see day 1.
   Activities: review and proceed with activities 1, 2, 3, 4, 5, and 6.

3. Man as body and soul; the relation between faith and reason
   Aim: to reinforce the teaching on God's existence; to perceive man as body and soul; to show the correct relationship between faith and reason.
   Activities: man as body and soul: see activities 7, 8, and 9; relation between faith and reason: see activities 10 and 11.

4. The attributes of God
   Aim: to reinforce the appreciation of God's perfections of presence, power, mercy, and knowledge.
   Activities: ask: "What are God's perfections?" and see activity 12.

5. The Trinity
   Aim: to present the doctrine of the Trinity.
   Activities: activities 13 and 14, quiz.

Notes:

CHAPTER 2

Divine Revelation

Background Reading for the Teacher:

Lawler, pp. 150−153, 165−167, 209−210, 543−549.
Hardon, pp. 29−50.

Aims:

The students should be able to identify and explain principal elements of divine revelation: the notion of revelation; Sacred Scripture, including inspiration and the Old and New Testaments; Sacred Tradition; the need for both Sacred Scripture and Sacred Tradition; the Creed; and the precise role of the Magisterium in interpreting Sacred Scripture and Sacred Tradition.

Materials Needed:

Pen, paper, blackboard, chalk, Bibles for all students, poster paper (optional), megaphone (optional), pictures of veiled women (optional), pictures of artwork depicting Bible scenes (optional).

Activities

1. Write on blackboard in large capital letters: GOD HAS SPOKEN TO US! Ask students: "What has God said to us?" Write on board: GOOD NEWS! Ask students: "*Why* has God spoken to us?" Try to draw out the answer: He has spoken to us because of his *goodness*. Ask them: "When was the last time you were dying to tell someone something wonderful that had happened to you?" Wait for replies. Give some examples: "If your mother just had a baby, what would you probably do?" (Tell your friends about it . . . good news!) "If you had just found out that you had been elected cheerleader, would you just hide this news from everyone?" (no) "If you got straight A's would you go home and show your parents the 'good news'?" (yes) "These examples show us something about goodness. Goodness always tries to spread itself. We say someone is good because he wants to share with us his happiness, much more than the best of friends on earth want to share joys with each other."

"How does God share his goodness? God shares with us his goodness through REVELATION." (Write it on the blackboard.) "What is revelation? 'Revelation' comes from a Latin word, *revelatio,* which means 'unveiling'." (Explain to the students that it is most helpful to know the roots of words.) "Have you ever been to an art show where a masterpiece was veiled? And then the special moment came for the unveiling? In ancient Eastern cultures it used to be the custom for a woman to wear a veil over her face, not just over her hair. Does anyone know why? She veiled her face in order to save her beauty for *only one person.* Who was this person? Her husband. Only her husband was permitted to unveil her face and gaze upon her beauty. This is like God and us. God's beauty, his truth, is unveiled to us through *revelation.*"

"Why do we need revelation? We go back to the veiled woman. When the veil covered her face, no one could see her beauty. Likewise, without revelation, there is a veil over our minds and our hearts. As we talked about in the last chapter, we can know that God exists, and we can know that there is a soul, but about God we can know nothing. Revelation takes the veil from our eyes so we can know better what God is like, what he wants us to do, for revelation is the unveiling of God to us."

2. Read Scripture on revelation: "Please open your Bibles. We are going to read together what God himself says about revelation. God is telling us, in Eph 1:9, that he is making known the mystery of his will; in 2 Pet 1:4, that through revelation we become sharers in God's divine nature; in Ex 33:11, that in revelation God addresses human beings as his

friends; and, in Bar 3:38, that through revelation God moves among men."

3. Compare Scripture and Tradition to human communication. "What is the value of words in communication? Let us pretend you have a very special friend who means the world to you. Now, what are two ways to communicate? For example, when your friend goes away for a vacation, how do you communicate?" (by letter, by writing) "On the other hand, when your friend is near you, how do you usually communicate?" (by talking) "Which do you like better, talking or writing? We can also compare Tradition and Scripture to learning. Would you like it if I never spoke to you, but just wrote my messages to you on the board? How did your parents teach you when you were little? Did they sit down and write letters to you on how to eat, how to brush your teeth, and so on? Of course not! They spoke to you and taught you by examples. Similarly, God does not communicate just through writing. He also communicates through Tradition." (Write on the board: TRADITION: THE SPOKEN WORDS AND ACTIONS OF GOD; and SCRIPTURE: THE WRITTEN WORD OF GOD.)

"Tradition and Scripture (the Bible) are both very important, just as both oral and written speech are very important in human communication. Please open your texts to p. 14. What is the Bible?" (the message of God put into writing under the inspiration of the Holy Spirit) "According to this paragraph, what is Tradition?" (Tradition delivers the word of God which was entrusted by Christ through the Holy Spirit to the apostles and their successors.) "This paragraph was taken from a book entitled *Vatican Council II Doc-*

23

uments. Vatican II was a recent meeting of the Pope, cardinals, and bishops."

4. "Let us go first to TRADITION." (Write it on the board.) " 'Tradition' comes from a Latin word, *traditio,* which means 'handing down'. Let us dramatize what it means to hand down." (Give your piece of chalk to the student in the first desk, and ask him to hand it down to the student behind him, and so on, until it reaches the student in the last desk.) "Tradition refers to the WORD OF GOD HANDED DOWN TO US FROM CHRIST AND THE APOSTLES." (Write on the board the definition of Tradition.)

"Which do you think came first, Tradition or Scripture? Tradition? First, as far as we know, Christ did not write books; he taught orally and by example. Second, his first apostles, for the first few years, taught the word of God orally and by their example. In fact, in Mt 28:20 Christ commanded his disciples to go and teach, not go and write."

"The reason it is important to emphasize this fact is that today there are many Christians who do not believe in Tradition; they believe only in the Bible. If we turn to the early years of Christ's teaching, we quickly see that Tradition came first."

Read what the Bible says on Tradition. "Please open your Bibles and turn to 2 Th 2:15. Clearly, St. Paul is urging the Church to hold firmly to Tradition (as in Jn 21:25). What are some examples of Tradition? One example is found on pp. 14 and 15. Who can find it?" (Give students some time to read.) "The answer is the CREED." (Write CREED on the board.) "What is the Creed? The Creed is the profession of faith, the statement of our basic beliefs as Catholic Christians. 'Creed' comes from a Latin word, *Credo,* which means

'I believe'. The Creed is very important as a chief example of Tradition. Some other examples are the statements of the Pope; the teachings of the Church, such as the one quoted for you in your book; the Mass and other parts of the Liturgy; and holy days."

5. Write SCRIPTURE on the blackboard. " 'Scripture' comes from a Latin word, *scriptura,* which means 'writing'." Write BIBLE on the blackboard. " 'Bible' comes from a Greek word that means 'the books'. What do you think the Bible means? The Bible is the written word of God. A 'scribe' comes from the same root as scripture; a scribe is one who would write, and he wrote in a room called a *scriptorium.* So, you see, scripture and Bible denote the idea of writing books."

"The Bible is the Book of Books. Just think how tremendous this book is: it contains all the important truths of God and man; in it, God appears, speaks, and acts; and it is the most widely read book in the world."

Discuss the history of the Bible in the Catholic Church. "Some people think that in the past Catholics did not like the Bible. This is not true. I will show you pictures of Bible scenes hung in churches that will show you how much the Catholic Church loved the Bible." (Show them pictures of such works as Michelangelo's Sistine Chapel, Moses, and David.) "Besides, the Church protected the books of the Bible from being burned when the barbarians tried to burn all the books. The monks saved the books. So, thanks to the Catholic Church, we have the Bible."

6. Write INSPIRATION on the blackboard. "What do you think inspiration is?" (Discuss with them their answers, pointing to what is correct and what is

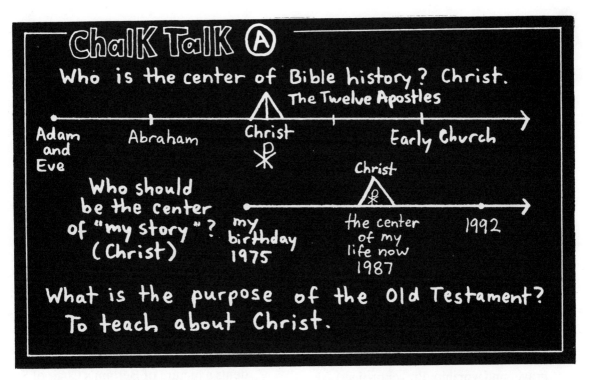

Chalk Talk Ⓐ

Who is the center of Bible history? Christ.

The Twelve Apostles

Adam and Eve — Abraham — Christ ☧ — Early Church

Who should be the center of "my story"? (Christ)

Christ ☧

my birthday 1975 — the center of my life now 1987 — 1992

What is the purpose of the Old Testament? To teach about Christ.

not.)" 'Inspiration' comes from a Latin word, *inspirare,* which means 'to breathe'. In inspiration God 'breathes forth' his word through human writers. What does your book say about inspiration? Can anyone find the definition?" (Give them some time.) "The answer is on p. 16: inspiration means that God moved certain men to write about him, and that he guided their minds as to what to record. How did God move these men to write about him? God is the primary author and these men are his *instruments.*"

"What does my chalk do? Who controls my chalk? The chalk is my instrument. Similarly, God, the author, writes his words through his evangelists and other sacred writers. God is like a sculptor, and the writers are like what?" (chisel) "God is like a writer and the evangelists are like what?" (pen, pencil, typewriter) "Can the Bi-

ble be wrong? No, the Bible cannot be wrong. By inspiration the Bible is preserved from all error."

Have the students look up the following Scripture passages on divine inspiration: Ex 4:15–16; Ezek 4:15–16, 38:1; Gal 3:8; 1 Cor 15:3–4; Eph 3:5; Col 1:26; 2 Th 2:13–15; Nb 11:25–26; Acts 3:22; 4:25; 28:25; Jer 1:9; 30:1–3; 36:1–3; Heb 1:1–2; Rom 3:21; 3:31; 2 Pet 1:19–21; 3:16; 2 Cor 3:7–8; 2 Tim 3:16; 1 Th 2:13.

7. *The Old Testament.* Write on the board: "The New Testament is hidden in the Old; the Old becomes clear in the New" (Vatican II, *Dei Verbum*). "In the Old Testament we see the story of salvation history."

"Who is the center of Bible history? Christ."

See chalk talk A.

"What is the purpose of the Old Testament? To teach about Christ. Turn to Lk 24:13–35." Assign students these parts: narrator, Cleopas and friend, Jesus. You may choose to have students act out this incident; the passage lends itself to dramatization.

After the students have read the passage, point out that Christ, "starting with Moses and the prophets explained to them the passages throughout the scriptures that were about himself." "This passage is considered the first 'Old Testament/Salvation History Lesson' and was taught by the Master Teacher himself. We study the Old Testament, then, to learn more about Christ and about his Father."

8. *Scripture in the Liturgy.* Show your students a Lectionary. Explain the important place the Bible has in our life of prayer and worship. Prayer project: ask your students to choose their favorite Scripture passage and write a meditation about it. Suggest that they tell why they like this particular passage. Some good passages are found in Proverbs, the Gospels, and the letters of St. Paul.

9. *The Magisterium.* Write MAGISTERIUM on the board. " 'Magisterium' comes from the Latin word *magister,* which means 'teacher'. What do you think magisterium means?" After some answers, direct the students to turn to p. 17. Write on the board: "MAGISTERIUM means the teaching authority of the Church." Ask the students to copy the definition in their notebooks. "Why is the Church called a 'Teacher'? What is a teacher supposed to do?" (to guide us, to show us the truth, to prevent us from making mistakes, etc.) "We need the Church, our teacher, to guide us to heaven; she teaches us the truth and

prevents us from making mistakes about our spiritual life, 'supernatural' mistakes."

Write POPE AND BISHOPS on the board. "Who are the successors of the apostles?" (the Pope and the other bishops of the world).

See chalk talk B.

Write INFALLIBILITY on the board. "Does anyone know what this word means? Turn to p. 17. Who can find the answer? 'Infallibility' comes from two Latin words, *in,* and *fallere,* which meaning 'cannot err'. Infallibility means the special gift belonging to the Pope and the bishops in union with the Pope which enables them to teach without error in faith and morals."

10. Display art: for example, show the students a picture of Bernini's Chair of St. Peter, which carries a beautiful illustration of the reality of infallibility: the dove, which represents the Holy Spirit, is above, directing the Pope, the successor of St. Peter.

11. Play a review game, as there are so many important vocabulary words in this lesson: bingo, peek-a-boo, or just a "vocabulary bee" are some good ones.

Lesson Plan for a One-day Presentation

1. Pray.
2. See activities 1–11, above.
3. Assign pp. 8–9 in the Activity Book.

Suggested Schedule for a Five-day Presentation

1. Revelation
   Aim: to define and understand by analogy the meaning of revelation.
   Activities: see activities 1 and 2.

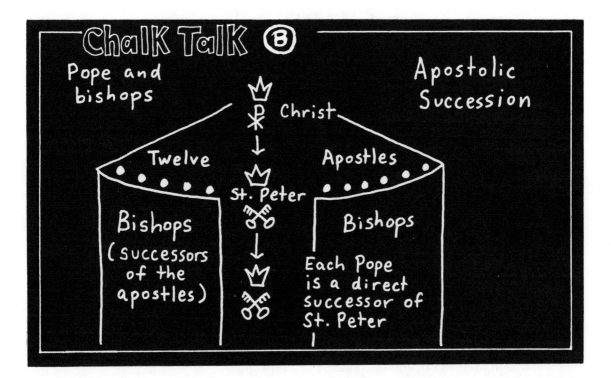

2. Scripture and Tradition
   Aim: to define and identify Scripture and Tradition as the source of revelation.
   Activities: see activities 3, 4, and 5.

3. Inspiration; the Old and the New Testaments
   Aim: to perceive the specific function of divine inspiration; to identify the purpose to the Old and the New Testaments and to memorize the books of the Bible.
   Activities: see activities 6, 7, and 8.

4. Magisterium; Pope and bishops, infallibility
   Aim: to define and explain the doctrines on the Magisterium, Pope and bishops, infallibility.
   Activities: see activities 9 and 10.

5. Test day
   Aim: to test the students' knowledge on Chapters 1 and 2.
   Activities: vocabulary test and short explanation questions.

CHAPTER 3

Creation

Background Reading for the Teacher:

Lawler, pp. 45–81.
Hardon, pp. 68–106.

Aims:

The students should be able to explain the doctrines contained in the Creation story: God as Creator; the notion of Creation; the goodness of all created things; the purpose of Creation; the creation of man; the first parents; the creation of man as male and female; the human person; the creation of the angels; the fall of the angels; the role of the guardian angels; the fall of Adam and Eve; the doctrine of original sin; and the promise of a redeemer.

Materials Needed:

Pen, paper, blackboard, chalk, Bibles, missalettes (optional).

Activities

1. Say as an opening prayer the Glory Be and as a short meditation of praise to God and his creation, the Canticle of St. Francis.

2. Ask the opening question, "Did God create the world because he was lonely, that is, there was no one else 'up there' in heaven? No, God created the world to show forth his goodness and to share with man his happiness. In no way was God 'lonely'."

   Write CREATE on the board. "What does 'create' mean?" (Give some time

for answers.) "Let us see what your book says. Please turn to p. 19. Who can find the answer?" (Write on the board: CREATE means to make something out of nothing.) "That means that before God created the universe, there was nothing material. Before God began his Creation there was nothing and no one but himself, the Family of the Trinity."

3. Discuss the meaning of "Genesis": " 'Genesis' comes from a Greek word meaning 'beginning'. Genesis, then, refers to what?" (Wait for answers.) "Yes, it refers to 'the beginning'. Why

do you think the people kept on telling one another the Creation story? In order to protect their faith in one God, to remind themselves that God created the world to show his love for mankind (unlike the stories of the pagan gods), and that everything God created was good. Some of the ancient peoples really believed that this world was all bad, that bodies, for example, were evil. The Creation story tells the truth. We, too, need to keep reminding ourselves of Catholic truths in a world that seems so pagan."

4. Read Gen 1:2. Then, as an art project, have the students "construct a picture of the Creation of the world, as you see it, or, rather, a Hebrew picture of the world. Your picture would illustrate how an ancient Hebrew would look upon the world."

   Discuss the word "good". "What does 'good' mean? What are some things that are good? Open your Bibles to Gen 1 and 2. How many times does the word *good* occur? Why?" (to emphasize that everything that God creates is *good*) "Think about some natural things that are good. Why are they good? Think about some people, about some man-made things that are good. Why are they good? When we see someone or something that is good, what should we think about?" From this reading have the students either write a newspaper report or do an art project on the "Beginning of the World."

5. Discuss man as God's greatest visible creation (see the chalk talk).

6. Review the concept of body and soul. "Remember when we were going over Chapter 1 a few weeks ago we talked about man as one who is composed of

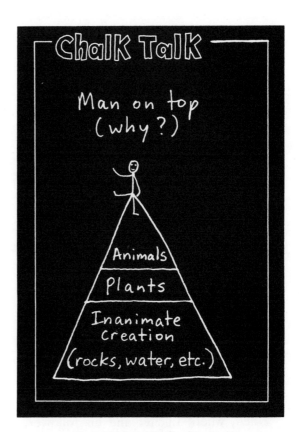

body and soul? What does that mean?" (Give them time to answer.) "Does the body need the soul? Does the soul need the body? In man, we can say yes: the body and soul go together. That is why on the last day we will be raised from the dead, our bodies united with our souls. The body is good and was made for the soul."

Write on the board BRASS = COPPER AND ZINC. "To have brass you must have both the elements of copper and zinc. Without the copper, you do not have brass; you have only _____. Without the zinc, you do not have brass; you have only _____. To have brass you must have _____ and _____, which are no longer individual elements, but are so united as to form a completely new compound.

Likewise, with the human person, you have _____ and _____ united to form the human being."

7. Discuss the creation of the angels. "God first created angels, which are pure spirits with intellect and will. God gave them a test to see whether they would choose to serve him or not. You see, even the angels had to have a test. Their test, says St. Augustine, was much quicker than ours because they have no bodies. (Our lives are one big test.) We do not know what this test was. We do know that some angels 'passed' the test and were then rewarded with the vision of God. One angel, the most brilliant, was named 'Lucifer', which means 'light bearer'. Lucifer 'flunked' the test because he would not serve God. He led other angels with him, so there was a battle between the good angels and the bad angels. The leader of the good angels is St. Michael. St. Michael threw Lucifer into hell, where Lucifer and his followers are right now."

"The name for a bad angel is 'devil'. The devils are very real. They try very hard to take us away from God so that we too will go to hell. The worst thing to do is to think that the devil is not real or not around. He is. Both the Bible and Tradition tell us so, and the Magisterium has reminded us of his existence."

8. Do an art project on Lucifer and Michael. Have the students write the mottoes of the good angels and the bad angels. The good angels: To serve God is to rule. The bad angels: I will not serve.

9. Discuss the concept of guardian angels. "God is so good that he gave us each an angel to watch over us and to protect us. What is this angel called?" (guardian angel) "Please turn to p. 21 and read the first paragraph in the second column." (Have a student read this paragraph aloud.) "What is the mission of the guardian angels?" (Give some examples of how the guardian angels can inspire and protect us: put holy thoughts into our minds; make us want to go to Mass; inspire us to go to confession; give us a special attraction for stories about saints; make us want to help others; urge us to choose friends who will help us to love God.) "The guardian angels also protect us physically. It is a good idea, for example, to pray to our guardian angels when we are traveling. God has given the angels real power to protect us, not only spiritually, but also physically."

Tell the story of St. John Bosco. "St. John Bosco is a great saint who helped teenage boys. He also defended the Church against people who did not believe in God. These people did not like St. John Bosco, so they tried to catch him off guard and beat him up. Each time they tried, however, a big dog would suddenly appear and frighten them away; the dog would then disappear. John Bosco called him 'Grey'. He firmly believed that Grey was his guardian angel in disguise."

10. *Prayers to the angels.* Make copies of the Prayer to St. Michael. Read it with your students, pointing out key doctrines: Michael the archangel; the battle between angels and devils; Satan fighting against us; the guardian angels fighting for us against Satan. Pray this prayer with your students every day until they know it by heart.

11. *The fall of man.* Explain how the test of man is one of obedience, an act of the will whereby one chooses to please God rather than self. "Read in your books silently on p. 21 the section under the title 'The Fall of Man'. What happened

to Adam and Eve? Why? What did Adam and Eve lose because of their disobedience to God? Continue reading silently on p. 22. Do all people have original sin? What is original sin? Was God unfair in punishing Adam and Eve and all their descendants?"

12. Read in the Bible on the fall of man. "Let us read together the accounts of the fall: Satan enters, uninvited. Satan enters our lives, too, uninvited (Gen 3:1). Eve dialogues with Satan instead of telling him to go away. Sometimes we, too, think about temptations instead of saying a quick No (Gen 3:2–3). Satan deceives; he always tries to make something bad look good (Gen 3:4–5). Eve feels attracted to the object of temptation (Gen 3:6). Eve coaxes Adam to join her. So often the devil tempts us through other people, especially our close friends who mean a lot to us; or we let the devil use us to tempt our friends to sin (Gen 3:6). Adam and Eve become aware of their nakedness—their loss of God's friendship— and they make excuses. They cannot bear to face God in their shame (Gen 3:7–8). When we do something wrong, we, too, tend to make excuses for ourselves and are afraid of God and of the priest in confession. We can compare Adam and Eve's fall to any sin we commit."

    As a class activity, ask the students to show how these steps are present in any sin someone their age can commit.

13. Role play a skit/interview with Adam, Eve, and the devil. Give the students some time to think of suitable lines for the interviews. Encourage them to excuse themselves and blame others, as Adam and Eve did.

14. *The Redeemer.* "God, who is infinitely loving, promised to save us from all the sad effects of sin. He promised a Redeemer. Let us read a description of this promise on p. 22." (Read aloud.) "Who is the woman described? Who will crush whose head? Who will strike at whose heel?" Have the class memorize Gen 3:15.

Lesson Plan for a One-day Presentation

1. Say the Prayer to St. Michael, or the Glory Be, as described in activity 1.

2. See activities 2–14, above.

3. Assign pp. 10–11 in the Activity Book.

Suggested Schedule for a Five-day Presentation

1. Creation
   Aim: to explain the doctrines underlying the Creation story, especially those of Creation and the purpose of Creation.
   Activities: see activities 2, 3, and 4.

2. Man and woman
   Aim: to identify man as a human person with intellect and free will.
   Activities: see activities 5 and 6.

3. Creation and fall of the angels
   Aim: to identify the nature of the angels and to point out the reality of Lucifer.
   Activities: see activities 7 and 8.

4. Creation and fall of the angels
   Aim: see day 3.
   Activities: see activities 9 and 10.

5. The fall of man and the promise of the Redeemer
   Aim: to understand the fall of man, on both the historical and spiritual levels, to know and to memorize the Scripture text of the promise of a Redeemer.
   Activities: see activities 11, 12, 13, and 14.

CHAPTER 4

God's Plan of Salvation

Background Reading for the Teacher:

Lawler, pp. 76–80, 235–237.
Hardon, pp. 78–82.

Aims:

The students should be able to identify the patriarchs Abraham, Isaac, and Jacob, and to point to their response of faith; to explain the meaning of "covenant"; and to perceive how Isaac and Joseph are prefigurements of Christ.

Materials Needed:

Pen, paper, chalk, blackboard, Bibles for all students, candy, missalettes.

Activities

1. As an opening prayer, say the Act of Faith. Explain the meaning of the Act of Faith. "What did we just tell God?" (We told him that we would believe him because he has told us what to believe, and he could never deceive us.) "What are things we should have faith in?" (the Eucharist, God's love for us, the Pope, and so on) "Do we always understand what we believe?" (No—consider the doctrine of the Blessed Trinity.) "Today we are going to see how some of the great men in the Old Testament were models of faith, believing even when they did not understand."

   Have the students read silently the story of Abraham on p. 26. "As you read, prepare to answer this question: Why is Abraham a model of faith?" (He believed that the Lord would give him many children even though he and his wife were very old; he obeyed when God called him; and he gave up his own land, home, and people out of faith in God.)

2. Write PREPARATION on the board. "What does this word mean? Can you give some examples? How about preparing for a party, for Thanksgiving, for a wedding, for a test? If you prepare well, what must you do? Now, God prepared the world for the coming of his Son. Do you think he would prepare

very carefully? Of course! If we try to prepare well for parties, how much more would God prepare the world for the coming of his beloved Son. The preparation of the world for the coming of Christ is called salvation history." Write SALVATION HISTORY on the board. "What is the name of the story of salvation history?" (the Old Testament)

3. Discuss the beginning of salvation history: the Covenant with Abraham. Explain the meaning of "covenant". Write COVENANT on the board. " 'Covenant' means a *serious, solemn agreement* between two parties, in this case, God and Abraham." (Write the definition on the board.)

   Make a covenant with the students. "Let us make a covenant: I promise not to make you stay after school, if you promise not to misbehave in class and to be respectful. I give you as a sign of our covenant this candy. Can you think of other serious covenants? One very serious agreement that most people make is the covenant of . . . ?" (marriage) "It is a very serious thing to make a covenant with one's spouse until death."

4. *The New Covenant.* "Christ came and made a New Covenant, signed with . . . (his Blood) "Where do we hear about this New Covenant?" (during the Mass, in the words of consecration) (Pass out missalettes.) "Who can find where 'covenant' is used? Let us read together."

   "What are the terms of the Covenant between Christ and us?" (God promises to free us from our sins and bring us to heaven. We promise to give up our sins, be baptized, and follow Christ's teachings in the Catholic Church. We renew this covenant during every Mass.)

"What is the difference between the Old and the New Covenants?" (The Old is between God and his Chosen People and promises a Redeemer; the New is between Christ and his Church and fulfills the promises of the Old Covenant.)

" 'Testament' is another word for . . ." (covenant). "That is why we call the books before Christ the Old Testament, and the books after Christ the New Testament."

5. Read aloud Gen 12:1–3. "What three commands did God give to Abram? What three promises? What virtue of Abram pleased God? Why?" (See Gal 3:7.) "How is Abraham like Mary, the Mother of Jesus, the Mother of God? Why?" Have the students make a chart showing how Abraham and Mary are alike.

6. "Why was Abram's name changed to Abraham?" (To show his new mission in life. This was common in salvation history. One often received a new name in order to signify his mission.) "Can you think of anyone else besides Abraham? We, too, take a special saint's name at baptism and at confirmation, choosing a patron or patroness whom we can imitate. What was your special saint's name given to you at baptism? At confirmation? If you have not yet been confirmed, what name will you choose?"

7. Tell the story of Isaac. Be sure to stress how dearly loved Isaac was as the only son of Abraham and Sarah. Or direct the students to read pp. 26–27 in their textbooks or Gen 22.

8. *Isaac as a type of Christ.* "Some of the Old Testament figures give us a foreshadowing, an idea what Christ would be like." (Write PREFIGUREMENT on the

board.) "Prefigurement means some person or event that happens before another to which it is similar in some way and to which it points. How is the sacrifice of Isaac a prefigurement of the sacrifice of Christ?" Make a chart or poster saying, "Isaac, type of Christ." "Write or sketch something to show all the ways that Isaac is like Christ, remembering that both were only sons and both were sacrifices."

9. Explain "sacrifice". Write SACRIFICE on the board. " 'Sacrifice' comes from two Latin words, *sacrum* and *facere,* meaning 'holy' and 'to make'. A sacrifice is a holy offering made to God. A real sacrifice is a holocaust." (Write HOLOCAUST on the board.) "Holocaust comes from words meaning 'whole, perfect offering'. When we give someone a gift, we show our love for that person by giving a new gift, not something that has been used or is broken. We wrap the gift in attractive paper, not old newspapers. The beauty and perfection of the gift show our love. For example, what did your father give your mother before they were married?" (an engagement ring)

"Therefore, a sacrifice must be something good. A real sacrifice is also something we love, not something we don't like. For example, it is not a sacrifice for most of you to give up doing your homework, is it? But, it would be a sacrifice to give up your special T.V. program, at least for many of you. We prove our love for someone not only by giving beautiful things, but by giving things that mean a lot to us that we are ready to give up nonetheless because of our love for the person to whom we are giving them."

"In the Old Testament, the people would give their best animals to God—healthy, young animals. Since the Hebrews made their living out of livestock, giving a perfect lamb or goat would mean a lot to them. Then, how great was the sacrifice of giving up one's only son, as Abraham did! We, too, must prepare to give up what is most precious to us, to offer God the best we have. In this way we show that we truly love him. What sacrifice do we give to God, or can give to him every day, one which is perfectly pleasing to him?" (The sacrifice of his only Son, a sacrifice offered in every Mass, one to which we unite our lives in his service)

"Make a list of sacrifices you, as seventh-graders, might offer. Remember that there are two requirements: each sacrifice must be important, even very precious to you, and it must be something good."

10. As an art project, make a plaque or a drawing featuring one of the following quotes from Mother Teresa of Calcutta: "Love is not love until it hurts"; "Sacrifice is the language of love."

11. Make a "family tree" of the patriarchs and their descendants mentioned in this chapter.

12. Have the students read silently the story of Joseph on pp. 27–28. Ask:
    a. "Why were Joseph's brothers jealous of him?"
    b. "What did they do to Joseph?"
    c. "How did Joseph get to Egypt?"
    d. "What happened to Joseph in Egypt?"
    e. "How are we sometimes like Joseph's brothers?"
    f. "List the ways in which we express jealousy of others."
    g. "How are some of us like Joseph, or could be like him?"
    h. "What are the remedies for jealousy?"

34

13. Discuss the sufferings of Joseph and the sufferings of Christ. "Joseph, like Christ, had many sufferings in his life." (read Gen 39:1–23) "Read quietly; then list the sufferings of Joseph that were like the sufferings of Christ." (Allow some time.) "Now let us see what you have listed." Direct one student to write on the board some of the sufferings the others name. Make a chart or poster showing how Joseph prefigured Christ.

14. As a skit, act out the story of Joseph (props: colored coat, sticks, old sheets). Direct the students to dramatize the story of Joseph. Have the narrator explain the spiritual meaning of this play. (God takes care of his people; jealousy results in many evils; virtue finally wins, etc.)

15. Instruct the students to read p. 28 to find out what happened four hundred years after Joseph died. Make a time line of the events of salvation history from the time of Abraham to the time of Moses.

16. *Providence.* " 'Providence' refers to God's loving care for his people. The story of Joseph is a good example of this beautiful Providence of the heavenly Father. Why?"

    Make a copy of the prayer of St. Thomas More for the students. "Why does St. Thomas refer to Joseph? How did Joseph's enemies actually do him good, rather than harm?" Read to the students the following prayer of St. Thomas More, written while he was a prisoner in the Tower of London.

Give me grace, good Lord,
to set the world at nought;

To set my mind fast upon thee,
and not to hang upon the blast of men's
    mouths.

To be content to be solitary;
Not to long for worldly company;

Little and little to cast off the world,
and rid my mind of all the business thereof;

Not to long to hear of any worldly things,
but that hearing of worldly phantasies
may be to me displeasant;

Gladly to be thinking of God;
Piteously to call for his help;

To lean on the comfort of God;
Busily to labor to love Him;

To know my own vility and wretchedness;
To humble and meeken myself
Under the mighty hand of God;

To bewail my sins passed
For the purging of them patiently to suffer
    adversity. . . .

To think my most enemies my best friends;
For the brethren of Joseph could never
    have
done him so much good with their love and
    favour
as they did with their malice and hatred.

Lesson Plan for a One-day Presentation

1. Pray the Act of Faith.

2. See activities 2–16, above.

3. Assign p. 12 in the Activity Book.

Suggested Schedule for a Five-day Presentation

1. Faith, salvation history, and covenant
   Aim: to identify the meaning of faith in one's own life; to explain how God prepared the world for the coming of his Son; to identify the meaning of covenant.
   Activities: see activities 1, 2, 3, and 4.

2. Abraham, sacrifice, and the story of Isaac

Aim: to understand why Abraham is our father in faith; to explain the true meaning of sacrifice; to review the story of Isaac.

Activities: see activities 5, 6, 7, 8, 9, and 10.

3. Jacob, Israel, and the story of Joseph

   Aim: to review the way God led his people; to identify the role of Israel and the way God cared for his people through Joseph.

   Activities: see activities 12, 13, and 14.

4. The role of Providence, the setting at the time of Moses, and review.

Aim: to identify the role of Providence in salvation history and in one's own life, to describe the setting at the time of Moses, and to review this chapter.

Activities: see activities 15–16.

5. Skit/project day

   Aim: to review through dramatizations and other projects the lessons learned in this chapter.

   Activities: see activity 14 and other activities above.

Notes:

CHAPTER 5

The Holy Prophet Moses

Background Reading for the Teacher:

Lawler, pp. 410–415.
Hardon, pp. 55–58, 288–290.

Aims:

The student should be able to describe and to explain the specific meaning of the call and the mission of Moses; to identify the symbolism of the Passover and the Exodus; to memorize and explain the Decalogue; to identify the role of the judges and the kings, especially the roles of Samuel, David, and Solomon; and to correlate the historical description of the Hebrew history in this chapter with the spiritual realities symbolized and foreshadowed.

Materials Needed:

Pen, paper, blackboard, chalk, Bibles, map of Old Testament history (optional); Holy Week missalettes.

Activities

1. Read Psalm 114 as an opening prayer. "This was probably written at the time of the Exodus and was thanking God for delivering his people from Egypt."

2. Introduce Moses. Write MOSES on the blackboard. "Last week we spoke about how names mean something special to God's chosen leaders. For example, why did Abram and Jacob have their names changes to Abraham and Israel? Today we are going to look at the holy prophet Moses, who received the Ten Commandments from God. Does anyone know what 'Moses' means? It comes from a Hebrew word, *masah*, which means 'to draw out'. Why do you think the name Moses was given to this prophet? Let us recall the story. Please turn to p. 29 in your text." As a writing assignment, have the students list the chief events in Moses' life and draw cartoons or pictures to illustrate their lists.

3. Discuss the call of Moses. Have students read silently the second column on p. 29. Ask:

a. "Why did God answer the prayers of the enslaved Hebrews?"

b. "What did God say to Moses? Why?"

c. "What did God reveal his own name to be?"

d. "What does the word 'Yahweh' mean?"

Have students read Ex 3:4–10, 15. Ask:

a. "What attracted Moses to the burning bush?" (It was blazing but not burned up.)

b. "What did God say to Moses as he began to approach the burning bush?" (to take off his shoes because he was standing on holy ground)

c. "Whose side was God on? Why?"
Easter Vigil reference: Pass out Holy Week missalettes, which are important for this lesson, because the Passover and the Exodus are included in the Holy Week Liturgy. "Please find a prayer about the burning bush in the Easter Vigil Liturgy." Point out how the Church uses the symbol of the burning bush to remind us of God's power and his eternity.

4. Write on the board: "Take off your shoes, for this is holy ground." "Why do you think God said this to Moses?" (to stress the adoration due to God) "There are some cloistered nuns who use this reference when explaining why they wear sandals, not shoes: because their whole life is centered upon adoring God." (You might need to write on the board "cloistered monks and nuns" and explain how important these men and women religious are to the Church.) "Because they are always walking in God's presence, they keep silence to be attentive to the Lord, except when they pray together."

Write down ways in which you can "take off your shoes" before the Lord. (kneeling reverently before the Blessed Sacrament, being very attentive during Mass, etc.)

5. Discuss the meaning of the word Yahweh. " 'Yahweh' is a most sacred word among devout Jews. Why? What does it mean?"(I AM, the name God revealed to Moses, which tells us that God is the source of all that exists) "He alone is eternal." (Write ETERNAL on the board.) "What does it mean?" (without beginning and without end) "God always was and always will be. Doesn't that 'boggle' your mind? Do you know why it is so hard for us to think about God's eternity? Because we are bound by time and space. We had a beginning. But God had no beginning and he will never end."

6. *The Passover of the Lord.* Write on the board: "Behold the blood of the Covenant which the Lord has made with you" (Ex 24:8). Explain that the word "Passover" comes from a Hebrew word, *pesakel* or *pascha,* which means "crossing over". "What is the feast of Passover? Turn to the second column on p. 30, to find out. Why was this feast called the Passover? What sign did God command his people to observe, a sign that they were a people sacred to him?"

7. *Paschal mystery.* "What is meant by the 'Paschal mystery' of the Lord? Why is it called Paschal mystery? To find the answer, turn to p. 31 in your text."

8. " 'Exodus' means 'flight'. *Ex* is a prefix, a Latin word meaning 'out of'. Can you think of some other words which use 'ex'?" (exit, extra, etc.) "What does the word exodus refer to? Read p. 31 to find out." *The Exultet.* "Read the Exultet found in your Holy Week missa-

lettes. Copy in your notes: (a) the part recalling the historical events in Egypt, and (b) references to the Redemption.''

9. *The people's complaints.* "The people began to complain against God and Moses. Let us see why by reading the first paragraph of the right-hand column on p. 31. Why were they complaining? How are the Hebrews' complaints like our complaints?'' Have the students compose a speech urging "your fellow Hebrews" (a) to follow Moses, and (b) to return to Egypt's Pharaoh.

10. *Heavenly manna.* "What is our heavenly manna?'' (the Eucharist) (Explain what Benediction is.) "In your missalettes turn to the page entitled 'Rite of Eucharistic Devotion'. Notice that the priest says, 'You have given us bread from heaven', and we reply, 'Having all sweetness within it'. Where does this reference come from?''

11. *The golden calf.* "While Moses was up on Mt. Sinai praying, the people grew tired and began complaining again. They melted their gold jewelry and molded it into an idol of a golden calf. What is an idol? What is the sin of idolatry? Turn to p. 31 to find the answer.''
    Our "golden calves". "When we read the story of the Hebrews' conduct, we might think, 'How stupid to ignore God, who took such good care of them, and adore a golden calf.' However, we might have our own golden calves—anything that takes us away from God or takes the place of God. What are some of the golden calves in our society? What might be the golden calves of seventh-graders? Let us list on the board some examples.'' Appoint one student to write the others' suggestions.

12. *Renewal of the Covenant.* "Even though the people had rebelled against God, they were sorry and God forgave them. Turn to p. 32 to see what God told the people. What was the agreement? Remember what a covenant is. What did Yahweh promise his people? What did the people promise Yahweh?''

13. *The Ten Commandments.* Check to see whether the students know the Ten Commandments. If not, assign their memorization.

14. *The Ten Commandments and examination of conduct.* "Turn to p. 34 to reread the Commandments; now turn to p. 171 to read the examination of conscience for these Commandments.'' Read and discuss the Commandments and the examination of conscience found in the text.
    After a class on the Ten Commandments, it might be helpful to have a penance service. The missalette usually has one.

15. As an art project, have the students make charts or posters focusing on one Commandment, showing how to practice it and how to break it. Have them draw little cartoons or sketches to illustrate their points. As a review game, describe a virtue or a sin that is linked with one of the Commandments. See who can guess first which one it is. Make up teams for competition.

16. If possible, get a map of Mt. Sinai showing Old Testament scenes. Point out Mt. Sinai, Egypt, the Red Sea, and the desert. Throughout this lesson, have the students work on a time line. After each section of study, ask them to extend it and add the characters or situation studied.

17. Review the meaning of sacrifice. "A sacrifice is (turn to the bottom of p. 32, left column) an offering to God of something that is precious to us." Talk about places of sacrifice. "Where were the sacrifices offered? For the answer, turn to p. 32." (on consecrated altars) "What was the purpose of offering sacrifice?" (To remind the people of the Covenant that their duty was to obey the law. The priests would ask God to forgive the sins of all the people.)

18. Discuss the meaning of "consecration". "According to your text, the word 'consecrate' means 'to set apart for the purpose of worshipping God'. 'Consecrate' comes from the Latin *con,* "with", and *secrare,* 'to set apart'. Thus someone or something that is consecrated is 'set apart'. For whom?" (God) "What are some of the things that are consecrated?" (altars, chalices, churches) "Which persons are consecrated?" (priests, religious brothers and sisters, bishops, popes, kings) "Why do we treat consecrated persons and things with respect?" (because of the purpose for which they were consecrated, not because of what they do)
    Consecrated things. "Which materials were required for the worship of God? See Ex 35 and 36. The best materials were always used for God's worship. Why?" (Only the best is fittingly offered to God; therefore, I must offer him my best, too.)

19. *Joshua.* "Who took over after Moses died? Why? Who was Joshua?" (See p. 32.) "Read and act out Jos 2 and Jos 6." The spies at Jericho and the help of Rahab make a dramatic story. Also, the battle at Jericho provides material for dramatization for the boys. The rest of the class might sing "The Battle of Jericho."

20. *Anointing.* "In the past athletes were anointed with oil to strengthen them. Similarly, kings were anointed to be blessed and strengthened in their task. That is why Samuel, the prophet, anointed Saul, the first king of Israel. When do we have anointings? (at baptism, confirmation, ordination, anointing of the sick) "What does 'anointing' mean? Anointing implies that chrism is used; thus "Christ" means "the anointed one", and this refers to the oil, or chrism, that is used.

21. *Psalms.* " 'Psalm' comes from a word meaning 'song'. Psalms were beautiful songs meant to be accompanied on the harp. David composed many psalms to praise God, to thank him, to ask him for help, or just to soothe troubled spirits. We still say/sing the psalms of David at Mass and in the Liturgy of the Hours." In the missalette find a psalm and read it together. Show the students the Liturgy of the Hours, and explain to them that the Church prays the psalms every day. Especially, the priests and religious pray the psalms in the name of the whole Church.

22. Assign p. 12 in the Activity Book, as homework (optional: memorization of Ps 23. Have the students prepare to recite it for the class.)

23. Use a map to show the division of the Two Kingdoms.

24. As an art project, have the students construct a miniature temple like that of Solomon, using the Bible for directions.

Lesson Plan for a One-day Presentation

1. Pray; see activity 1, above.

2. Activities 2–24.

40

3. Assign pp. 13–14 in the Activity Book.

Suggested Schedule for a Five-day Presentation

1. Introduction to Moses
   Aim: to identify the specific meaning of the call and mission of Moses, and to perceive spiritual parallels in our own lives.
   Activities: see activities 2, 3, 4, and 5.

2. Continuation of the story of Moses
   Aim: see above.
   Activities: see activities 2, 3, 4, and 5.

3. Passover and Exodus
   Aim: to identify the symbolism of the Passover.
   Activities: see activities 6, 7, 8, 9, and 10.

4. Exodus and the Ten Commandments
   Aim: to identify the symbolism of the Exodus and to review the Ten Commandments.
   Activities: see activities 8, 9, 10, 13, 14, 15, and 16.

5. Review: Renewal and sign of the Covenant, Joshua, the judges, and the kings.
   Aim: to review the previous lesson; to identify and describe the Ark of the Covenant; to explain the notion, both historical and personal, of "sacrifice" and "consecrate"; to identify and explain the roles of Joshua, the judges, and the kings; to identify the psalms.
   Activities: see activities 12, 17, 18, 19, 20, and 21.

Notes:

CHAPTER 6

God's Special Spokesmen: The Prophets

Background Reading for the Teacher:

Lawler, pp. 78–79, 203–204, 448–449.
Hardon, pp. 73, 206–297.

Aims:

The students should be able to identify the meaning, mission, and manner of the Old Testament prophets; to explain the precise roles and importance of Elijah, Elisha, Isaiah, and John the Baptist; to memorize the names of the four major prophets (Isaiah, Jeremiah, Ezekiel, Daniel).

Materials Needed:

Pen, paper, blackboard, chalk, text, Bibles; optional: costumes for skits, play microphones, poster paper, colored pens/crayons, Advent missalettes, lectionary, wads of paper, stuffed animals, bread, jars of water.

Activities

1. Pray a Hail Mary and add "Mary, Queen of Prophets, pray for us." Tell the students: "We prayed to Mary, Queen of Prophets, because today's class is about the prophets. Turn to p. 169 of your text, to the beautiful prayer called 'The Litany of the Blessed Virgin Mary'. Who can find the title 'Queen of Prophets'? As you can see, Mary is everybody's Queen, but since she is in a special way the Queen of Prophets, we ask her to help us today."

2. "Does anyone know what prophets are?" (Write PROPHETS on the blackboard.) "Once again, we go to the root of the word: 'prophet' comes from the Greek *pro* and *phanai,* which mean 'to speak before'; so 'prophesy' means 'speak on behalf of someone'." A prophet, then, is a person who speaks in God's name as a teacher to help and

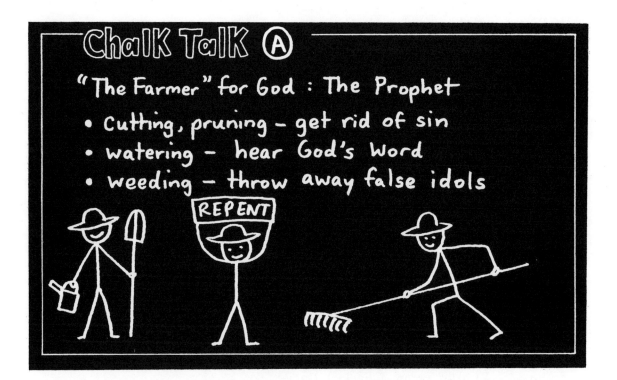

Chalk Talk A

"The Farmer" for God : The Prophet
- Cutting, pruning — get rid of sin
- watering — hear God's Word
- weeding — throw away false idols

REPENT

guide God's people. Turn to p. 35. What do most people think a prophet is? What is the definition your book gives—one different from the notion most people have?" (A prophet is someone chosen by God to speak a message from him to his people.) "The ultimate mission of the prophets was to prepare for the coming of Christ."

See chalk talk A. "The prophets were like farmers and gardeners for God. In what way? They cultivated God's garden so that it would be beautiful for his Son. Were you ever asked by your parents to spend some time mowing the lawn, pruning, weeding, watering, and so on, because you were expecting company? God, like the head of a family, sent his gardeners, the prophets, out to weed and cultivate the ground for a beautiful garden ready for his Son."

3. Direct the students to draw a "garden" with God's gardeners, the prophets, pruning, weeding, cultivating. Write down the specific kind of pruning, weeding, and cultivating done by these gardeners: messages of repentance, reminders of God's love, warnings, etc.

4. Use mnemonics to help the students memorize the major prophets. "This is an example: Isaiah, Jeremiah, Ezekiel, Daniel. Take the first letter of each of the names. What do we have? I J E D. Make up a nonsense ditty or phrase, such as 'I Just Eat Doughnuts.' "

5. Talk about Elijah and Elisha. Have the students read silently the section "The Prophets Elijah and Elisha" on pp. 36–37. Write on the board these questions for them to answer:
a. For what was Elijah most famous?

b. What miracle happened on Mt. Carmel?

c. What did Elisha see happen to Elijah?

d. What was one of Elisha's miracles?

e. Why are Elijah and Elisha especially important to the Catholic Church?

6. *The Carmelites.* Write CARMELITES on the board. "Have you ever heard of Carmelites? (Don't confuse the word with caramel candy!) The Carmelites are a very old and special cloistered order." (Write CLOISTERED on the board.) "Of all the cloistered orders, the Carmelites are one of the strictest; they pray a great deal, keep silence, and practice many penances. Where do you think they got the name 'Carmelites'?" (Mt. Carmel was where Elijah performed his miracle by praying to God.) "As Elijah discovered that God was not in the mighty wind, or the raging fire, but in the gentle breeze (1 Kings 19:12–13), the Carmelites discover God in silence. They seek God, not just for themselves, but for the whole Church; they pray to God for all of us. We need them. Why?"

7. *Isaiah.* Write ISAIAH on the board. "What is Isaiah famous for? Turn to p. 36." Read some of the prophecies of Isaiah: Virgin Birth (Is 7:14); a light has shone (Is 9:1); Prince of Peace (Is 9:5–6; and shining in glory (Is 60:1–3). Discuss what these prophecies mean. "How do these passages remind you of Christmas?"

Prophecies and fulfillment. "Let's find the fulfillment of the prophecies by looking in Lk 1:26–36; 2:29–32; 2:8–14; and Mt 2:1–6." Have the students read Isaiah's prophecies on p. 36 and then write them under the heading "Prophecies about the Messiah." In a column to the right have them sketch a picture or write a word picture. Have them explain to what this prophecy refers.

8. See chalk talk B. "Why do you think I have John the Baptist as a bridge? Find the answer on p. 37." (St. John is the last of the Old Testament's prophets, and the only one to witness the fulfillment of the prophecies. It is John who sees and points out Christ to the people.) Read the description of St. John from pp. 37–38. For the reading select a narrator, an angel, the Holy Spirit, and the voice of St. John the Baptist. Ask these questions on the reading about John the Baptist:

a. "Who is older, John or Jesus?"

b. "What is a forerunner?"

c. "What is a herald?"

d. "What is the meaning of 'repent'?"

e. "Why is John called 'the Baptist'?"

f. "How did St. John die?"

9. *John the Forerunner.* "How do the two words 'fore' and 'runner' indicate to us the meaning of the word? How is John the Baptist a forerunner?"

Herald. "How many of you have seen pictures showing a king's royal herald? What does this herald do?" (blows a horn to attract attention) "A herald speaks in the name of the king, giving the king's messages, not his own."

10. Tell the students to write what they imagine John the Baptist might have been thinking during his imprisonment. (See also Mt 11:1–6.)

Lesson Plan for a One-day Presentation

1. Pray as directed in activity 1.

2. See activities 2–10, above.

3. Assign p. 15 in the Activity Book.

Suggested Schedule for a Five-day Presentation

1. Role of the prophets
   Aim: to identify and explain the precise mission of the prophets.
   Activities: see activities 1, 2, 3, and 4.

2. Role of the prophets, continued; kinds of prophets
   Aim: see day 1; also, to memorize the major prophets.
   Activities: see activities 1, 2, 3, and 4.

3. Elijah and Elisha
   Aim: to identify and explain the roles of Elijah and Elisha.
   Activities: see activities 5 and 6.

4. Isaiah
   Aim: identify and explain the role of Isaiah and his prophecies.
   Activities: see activity 7.

5. John the Baptist; review
   Aim: to identify the role of John the Baptist; to explain how we need "John the Baptists" today.
   Activities: see activities 8, 9, and 10.
   Review of Part One.

PART TWO

God Becomes Man

CHAPTER 7

Our Lord and Savior Jesus Christ

Background Reading for the Teacher:

Lawler, pp. 81–97.
Hardon, pp. 110–113, 122–144.

Aims:

The student should be able to identify and explain the reason for the Incarnation; to describe the Old Testament preparation for Christ; to analyze the meaning of the Incarnation and Mary's role in the Incarnation; to meditate upon the example of Mary's humility and obedience in the Annunciation; to define the hypostatic union; to know that Christ is both God and man; and to identify early heresies about the Incarnation.

Materials Needed:

Pen, paper, blackboard, chalk, texts, Bibles (optional), old sheets for costumes, poster paper and colored felt pens, pictures of the Annunciation scene, recordings of Gregorian chant and polyphony of the *Ave Maria,* pictures of the Nativity, missalettes for the Christmas season, record player.

Activities

1. Pray the Angelus (p. 168 in text). Tell the students the reason for praying the Angelus: it reminds us of the central Mystery of our faith, the Incarnation. Write INCARNATION on the board.

2. "We all believe God became man, but why? Turn to p. 41 in your texts." (God promised Adam and Eve that he would send a Redeemer, someone who would make up for the effects of sin and the consequent separation between God and man, between the Creator and the creature.) Using the chalkboard, explain the need for the God-man: God, not man, had to make up for man's sin. List and discuss the following:
   a. "Redeem" means "buy back".

b. Why could only God, not man, make up for sin?

c. Write on the board: An offense is proportionate to the one offended.

d. Analogy: "Let us say that Tom, in a very bad mood one day, hit his little sister. But then, Tom also went over to his parents, tore up his father's newspaper, threw a plate, and said some ugly things to both parents. Which is worse, Tom's striking his sister or his offenses to his parents?" (Because his parents represent God to him, they deserve more respect than his sister; therefore the offenses against them are more serious.) "Can anyone relate this story to the relationship between God and man?" (God is infinitely worthy of respect because he is infinitely holy.)

3. Analysis of the meaning of reparation. "Let us say that Tim stole $5 from you. How much would you want back?" (at least $5; perhaps more to make up for the offense and the inconvenience) "If he stole $25? If he stole $100? Or, since he was gaining confidence in his ability "to get away with it", he managed to steal from the bank $1,000 or $10,000? If you owned this bank, how much would you expect back? This story gives us a clue about how much man owes God. Sin is an offense against God, whose dignity is infinite. How much must be paid back to God for sin?" (an infinite amount) "Could any man pay back an infinite amount to God?" (Only the God-man, one who is himself infinite in dignity and could, therefore, atone for an infinite offense. So God had to be the victim for sin.)

See chalk talk A.

"Man, too, had to make up for man's sin." Analogy: "Let us pretend that

some seventh-graders pulled the fire alarm and caused the entire school to lose time and money. Should the first-graders be punished? The fourth-graders? Which grade?" (the seventh) "Let us imagine that the principal said that if the guilty one would admit to his action and take his punishment for the offense, no one else would have to suffer; but if no one volunteered the truth, everyone in the school would have to attend classes for an extra month. Who should volunteer?" (the guilty one: the one who committed the crime, a seventh-grader) "In like manner, because man sinned, it was necessary that man suffer for the offense of sin. This is why God became man: man sinned; man needed to make up for the sin."

4. *Prophecies of the Messiah.* Analogy to a foggy, dark night: "On a dark, foggy night you are walking, when all of a sudden, you detect someone moving. As he gets closer, you can see what he looks like. This is like the prophecies and Christ. How?"

   Analogy to a picture of a friend whom one has not seen for a long time: "If your friend whom you have not seen in a long time left with you a picture of himself, it helps to remind you of what he looks like, doesn't it? The prophecies are like pictures of Christ, graphic portrayals of the Suffering Servant of Yahweh. To see what Christ would be like, let us turn to p. 41 and find specific prophecies."

5. *The Incarnation of the Lord; the Annunciation.*
   "Turn to page 163. Let us read the Angelus together. This prayer, adapted from Lk 1:26–38, tells us of Mary's Yes to God. Mary's Yes to God can be compared to the response to a proposal of

marriage. What are the steps in a proposal?"

	Man-made	*God-made*
a. The proposal	Will you marry me?	Will you be the Mother of the Messiah?
b. The answer	Yes.	*Fiat.* Yes, God. Be it done to me as you will.
c. The result	Friendship, wedding, children.	The conception of Christ the God-man, the Redeemer.

6. Write INCARNATION on the board. "What does Incarnation mean? Not the birth of Christ! Why? Because the birth of Christ took place nine months after the Annunciation. It means the conception of Christ; it took place as soon as Mary said Yes to God. What was the most important event in human history? The Incarnation. Who determined the entire course of human history? Mary, because the central event of human history awaited her Yes. This 'yes' is called Mary's *fiat. Fiat* is a Latin word meaning 'let it be done'. Mary wanted only God's will, she cooperated perfectly with him, and Jesus was conceived within her."

7. "What virtues does Mary teach us?" (obedience and humility) "Her *fiat* expressed her obedience, her acceptance of God's will. Let us make a list of what our *fiats* might be. Let us strive to be like Mary, always saying Yes when we know what God wants of us. The greatest event in human history occurred be-

cause of Mary's obedience. Does this fact teach us a lesson? It teaches us that great things will happen when we obey God. We do not always know, as Mary did in this case, what will happen, but we know that God 'makes all things work together for the good of those who love him' (Rom 8:28). We must trust God.''

8. Bring to class some masterpieces of medieval and Renaissance periods to show how Christian artists took the Annunciation as one of their favorite themes. "Why do you think that the Annunciation was a favorite theme for artists?"

9. Teach the students to sing the Gregorian *Ave Maria*. Explain the meaning of the Latin and the importance of Gregorian chant in the life of the Church. Play for the students the *Ave Maria* in both chant and polyphony. A particularly beautiful rendition is Victoria's *Ave Maria*. After the students have heard it, ask them to make some spiritual reflections.

10. "The gap between a man and worm is not so great as the gap between God and man. Both man and worm have a body; both are creatures; both will die. But God is the Creator, pure Spirit, infinitely greater than the greatest of his creatures. Yet, God became a man, took for himself a body that he created, so that he could be like us and help us, when we couldn't help ourselves. How much we should thank God for the great gift of the Incarnation of the Son of God!" See chalk talk B.

11. Read the Creed. "Take out your missalette. Who can find the Creed, the Profession of Faith? What is the reference to the Incarnation? Do you know on which feast days we kneel at those words?" (Christmas and Annuncia-

tion) "Why?" Write the phrase "ET HOMO FACTUS EST" on the board. "This is the Latin of these words of Creed: 'The Word was made flesh'.''

12. "Why did the Second Person of the Blessed Trinity become man? Turn to p. 42 to find out. God became man to share our life (when you love someone, you want to share his joys and sorrows); to give us an example; to free us from original sin so we can become children of God again; to reveal the Blessed Trinity."

Write on the board St. Bernard's statement: The sound of words is a hand-clap; the sound of example is thunder. "Why was Christ's most effective teaching done by his example? How can we imitate him?"

Make a chart to show how Christ taught the virtues by his example. In the first column list Christ's virtues; in the second, the Gospel references; in the third, ways in which we can imitate Christ.

13. "Hidden life of Christ? What is meant by the hidden life of Christ? How long did it last? Turn to p. 42, second column, to find the answers." Ask:
    a. "What kind of life did Jesus live with Mary and Joseph?"
    b. "Why did he live that way?" (to teach us that we can please God very much by doing ordinary things well, such as working and helping at home and leading a virtuous family life)
    c. "Why was this part of his life called 'hidden'?"
    d. "What can we do to imitate Christ in his hidden life?"

14. *God and man.* "Turn to pp. 42–43, references that show that Jesus is truly God and man. Make two columns to list your findings:"

True God	True Man
Mt 3:17 (p. 42)	He felt hungry and thirsty (Lk 4:2).

15. *The hypostatic union.* "Turn to p. 43 to find the definition of hypostatic union." See chalk talk C.

16. *The name of Jesus.* " 'Jesus' means 'Savior'; it is a sacred name (Phil 2:10), a name that frightens the devils, for all hell trembles at the mention of this holy name. We should always say the name of Jesus devoutly; we should say it of-

ten, on our lips and in our hearts, because Jesus is our Redeemer and Lord, and through his name we gain grace."

17. As an art project, have the students do sketches of the following:
   a. the Annunciation.
   b. a scene from the life of Christ showing that:
      1. he is God;
      2. he is man.
   Description of Jesus. There are no photographs or drawings of Jesus made by someone who knew him. (There is the Shroud, which shows a negative imprint of the Man of Sorrows, Jesus' body in death.) From the Gospel accounts of Jesus' words and actions, reflect upon his appearance, speech, actions, and thoughts; emphasize especially the following:

   a. his appearance
   b. his facial expressions
   c. his tone of voice
   d. his choice of words
   e. his tenderness and compassion
   f. his manliness
   g. signs of his divinity

   "Write a summary, a description of Christ, according to your reflections for yourself and for someone you would like to see become closer to Christ (a fallen-away Catholic, an unbeliever, etc.)

18. *Heresies about the Incarnation.* Write on the board HERESY. "A heresy is a false teaching about the Catholic faith." (for example, to deny that Jesus is God; to deny that he is truly man; to deny that Mary was conceived immaculate or that she is the Mother of God; to deny that Jesus is truly present in the Holy Eucharist, body, blood, soul, and divinity; to deny that Jesus gave St. Pe-

ter and all the popes the gift of infallibility to protect them from error and to protect the faith of the people) "The cause of heresies is basically pride. Sometimes people want to understand fully the mysteries God has revealed, but only God understands them fully. We should seek to know more and more what God has revealed so as to appreciate it more and to be more grateful, but mysteries remain mysteries. We can be sure that we are being taught the truth when we listen to what the Magisterium of the Church is teaching us."

19. a. "Turn to p. 43 to find out what the heresy of Docetism is. The Docetists said that Jesus only seemed to be a man. Why did those people believe this way?" (because they thought the body evil) "What does Genesis teach about the body? Everything that God created, the body included, was good."
   b. "Turn to p. 43 to find out what the Arian heresy is. What is Arianism? How is the Arian heresy the opposite of Docetism? The Arian heresy taught that Jesus Christ was only a man, but not God. Arianism is a very interesting heresy because, as your text tells you, it influenced even the bishops and priests; only a few of them and some of the devout lay people kept the faith of the Church. The bishop who led the fight against the Arians was St. Athanasius. He brought the matter to the Pope, who called a council. This story shows us that we must know our faith very well and be ready to defend it."
   c. "Turn to pp. 43 and 44 of your text to find out whether the two heresies of Arianism and Docetism can be found even today." Make a chart on

the two leading heresies about the Incarnation.

Heresy	Definition	Errors
Arianism		
Docetism		

Lesson Plan for a One-day Presentation:

1. Pray the Angelus; see activity 1, above.

2. See activities 2–19.

3. Assign pp. 16–17 in the Activity Book.

Suggested Schedule for a Five-day Presentation

1. Preparation for the Incarnation; necessity of the Incarnation
   Aim: to identify and explain the necessity for the Incarnation; to describe the Old Testament prophecies and other preparations for Christ.
   Activities: see activities 1, 2, 3, and 4.

2. The Incarnation of the Lord; the Annunciation
   Aim: to analyze the meaning of the Incarnation and Mary's role in it; to meditate on the example of Mary's humility and obedience; to appreciate Catholic culture (art and music) on themes of the Annunciation.
   Activities: see activities 5, 6, 7, and 8.

3. The Incarnation
   Aim: to appreciate the humility of Our Lord in the Incarnation; to identify the importance of imitating Jesus Christ.
   Activities: see activities 9, 10, 11, and 12.

4. The hypostatic union and the hidden life
   Aim: to correlate the example of the hidden life with our life; to define the doctrine of the hypostatic union; to explain how Christ is truly God and truly man.
   Activities: see activities 13, 14, 15, 16, and 17.

5. Heresies on the Incarnation
   Aim: to identify and explain the early heresies on the Incarnation.
   Activities: see activities 18 and 19.

CHAPTER 8

The Saving Mission of Jesus

Background Reading for the Teacher:

Lawler, pp. 112–124, 162–173.
Hardon, pp. 117–122.

Aims:

To identify Christ's saving mission, his manifestation of the Blessed Trinity, and his triple role of prophet, priest, and king.

Materials Needed:

Pen, paper, blackboard, chalk, Bibles (optional), poster paper, colored pens, recording of Handel's *Messiah*, record player.

Activities

1. Pray the Acts of Faith, Hope, and Love found on pp. 167–168. "What have we just offered to God? Turn to p. 47, the second column. We have worshipped God by reciting these prayers. Who can find a description of this worship?"

2. "Some people imagine God as a policeman holding a big stick! God is infinitely just, but he is also infinitely loving and compassionate" (Jn 3:17). Why did God send his only Son into the world?" (to save the world) "Prove that Jesus did everything out of love for his Father. You can find the answer on pp. 46–47."

3. "Prove that Jesus revealed to us the inner life of the Blessed Trinity. You can find the answers on pp. 46–47." See chalk talk A.
"Think of the person you love most in the world. If that person asked you to do something very difficult, but something that would make him or her very happy, could you say no? It is very difficult to say no to someone you love. Why? How is this like Jesus and his Father?"

4. Our imitation of Christ. "Jesus always did what pleased his Father. For us,

Chalk Talk Ⓐ

too, the will of God is most important in our lives." List on the chalk board some of the things seventh graders can do to please God.

5. Write TEACHER, PRIEST, KING on the board. "On a piece of paper, write the associations or words that come to your mind when you think of 'a very good teacher'. Then write the words that come to your mind when you think of 'a very good priest'. Then write the words you associate with 'an excellent king'."

"How is Christ the best of all teachers? the best of all priests? the best of all kings? Why do we have teachers? priests? kings? Why do you think the Father sent his Son to be a teacher? a priest? a king?"

"List the following titles for three columns: Jesus Christ, Teacher; Jesus Christ, Priest; Jesus Christ, King. Now read quietly on pp. 47–48. Then fill in your answer in the appropriate columns." (You might make worksheets in advance for this assignment.)

6. Make a poster or just use a paper for the following: Christ the Teacher; the Magisterium; me. Tell the story of Mary of Bethany, who sat at the feet of Jesus listening to him teaching.

7. "What is the role of a priest? See Heb 5:1–5." See chalk talk B.

8. "Compose a chart on how Christ is Priest, how the ordained priest acts like Christ, and how you share in the 'common priesthood' (column titles: Christ the Priest; ordained priests; me)."

9. "Make a chart of the worldly kingdom and the spiritual Kingdom; describe by word or picture. Make sure you show the differences."

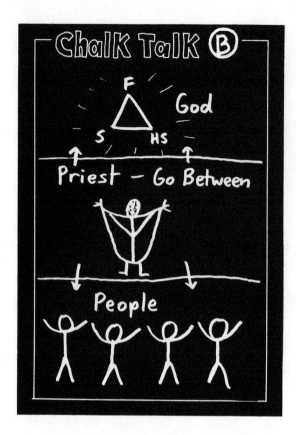

10. Play the "Hallelujah Chorus" of Handel's *Messiah*. Note for the class the veneration shown when the chorus sings, "King of kings and Lord of lords . . ." Discuss genuflections. "In olden times, how did people show respect for their king?" (by genuflecting) "Let us practice making reverent genuflections." (right knee to the left instep; with back erect; your attention on the tabernacle where Christ the King is present for your visit)

11. "In ancient times, what happened to people who were about to be teachers, prophets, or kings? They were _____." (anointed) "Why were they anointed?" (Anointing was a sign of God's blessing on their great and special mission.) "Why, then, is Christ called the 'Anointed One'?" (He is the supreme Teacher, Priest, and King.)

12. Show pictures of Christ the Teacher, a common theme among the early Christians; of Christ the Priest; of Christ the King.

13. "Make a chart listing our duties to Christ who is our Teacher, Priest, and King."

Teacher	Priest	King
We must listen to him.	We must share in his eucharistic Sacrifice and often ask his help.	We must show him respect by our reverent genuflections.

Lesson Plan for a One-day Presentation

1. Pray; see activity 1, above.

2. See activities 2–13.

3. Assign pp. 18–19 in the Activity Book.

Suggested Schedule for a Five-day Presentation

1. Christ's saving mission
   Aim: to identify Christ's saving mission and his revelation of the Trinity; to perceive his love for the Father's will; to imitate his love for the Father's will.
   Activities: see activities 1, 2, 3, and 4.

2. Christ the Teacher
   Aim: to identify Christ's role as Teacher.
   Activities: see activities 5, 6, 11, 12, and 13.

3. Christ the Priest
   Aim: to identify Christ's role as Priest.
   Activities: see activities 5, 7, 8, 11, 12, and 13.

4. Christ the King
   Aim: to identify Christ's role as King.

Activities: see activities 9, 10, 11, 12, and 13.

5. Christ, the Anointed One: Teacher, Priest, King
   Aim: to identify in general the three-fold role of the Anointed One.
   Activities: see activities 11, 12, and 13.

Notes:

CHAPTER 9

The Priesthood of Jesus

Background Reading for the Teacher:

Lawler, pp. 434–441; 457–459.
Hardon, pp. 136–137, 446; 521; 553.

Aims:

To identify the priesthood of Jesus by noting the Old Testament references concerning preparation for Christ's priesthood; to explain the three things required for every sacrifice (priest, victim, altar); and to analyze how Christ is the perfect priest and victim on the altar of the Cross on Calvary.

Materials Needed:

Pen, paper, blackboard, chalk, Bibles, texts; missalettes (optional).

Activities

1. Pray the *Memorare* on p. 170. Ask the students to offer their prayers for priests. "We are going to study 'The Priesthood of Jesus'. Let us continue to do what we did to open this class: pray for priests. Priests, who stand in the Person of Christ, are to remind us of Christ the High Priest."

2. "What is a priest?" (Allow time for responses.) "A priest is one who offers sacrifice." (Write this definition on the board.) "In other Christian denominations there are ministers, preachers, but not priests, not men who offer Christ's Sacrifice on behalf of the people."

3. "What is a sacrifice?" (As a repetition, use the lesson in Chapter 4.) Write SAC RIFICE on the board. " 'Sacrifice' comes from two Latin words, *sacrum* and *facere,* which mean 'holy' and 'to make'. A sacrifice, then, is a holy offering to God, a gift to God."

   "But God does not need our sacrifices! He is God! That is correct in one sense. God is infinitely perfect and does not need our sacrifices. But in another way, our sacrifices symbolize something God cannot have without our consent: our love."

   "A sacrifice is similar to giving gifts to people we love. The gift proves that we are truly thinking about our friend, especially when the gift is clearly one that required us to sacrifice to buy it or make it. Do you remember making cards for Mothers' Day when you were in second or third grade? Could you have sold them for much money because they were so beautiful? Of course not! Your mother deeply appreciated your card because it expressed your love for her and because it clearly showed that you had spent a lot of time making it. Likewise God is pleased with our sacrifices, not because he needs them, but because they show our love and gratitude. List some sacrifices that you as seventh-graders can offer to God."

4. "Turn to p. 49 in your book, 'Offering Sacrifices to God'." Ask:
   a. "Why did God accept Abel's offering but not Cain's?"
   b. "What kind of sacrifices please God?"

5. "Please turn to Gen 4:1–8 and read it."
   a. "What does the Bible say about how God looked on Cain's offering?"
   b. "What happened to Cain when God did not accept his offering?"
   c. "Anger joined with sadness at someone else's good fortune is very bad. Because Cain was angry and sad over Abel's good fortune, God pointed out to him what would happen: 'If you are ill-disposed, is not sin at the door like a crouching beast . . .' What lesson can we learn from this story?"

6. "Please turn to Gen 8:20–22. Did God tell Noah to offer a sacrifice?" (No, Noah did it because he knew it was the right thing to do.) "What kind of sacrifice did Noah offer?" ("Choosing from all the clean animals and all the clean birds he offered burnt offerings on the altar"—he chose the best.) "Was God pleased? Do we have proof of his

pleasure?" (Yes, God was pleased; he promised that he would never again destroy the world by flood. God made a covenant with Noah to prove his promise.)

7. "The offering of sacrifices has another purpose besides that of showing our gratitude to God. Turn to p. 49, second column, to find that purpose." (Offering sacrifices shows our sorrow for sin.)

8. Review briefly the history of the Old Testament priesthood:
   a. Age of the patriarchs: at this time the father of the family offered sacrifices to Yahweh.
   b. Time of Moses: God established through Moses the Levites, a special group of men who would offer sacrifices on behalf of themselves and all the people.
   c. Christ: Christ is the priest who offers sacrifice for all the people.

9. "Turn to p. 49. The picture you see was painted by Raphael; it is called 'Noah'. Why? What do you see in this picture?" (Someone standing before an altar and raising his hands in prayer. This person is Noah. There are others: man with knife slaughtering an animal; another man holding a goat.)

   "This painting shows us the three things necessary for offering sacrifice. You can identify them by turning to p. 50." (The three necessary things are priest, victim, and altar.) "Who is the priest in the picture? The victim? The altar? When we offer sacrifices to God, how must we offer them? Can you explain the three points at the top of page 50?"
   a. "A pure, a sinless heart, a heart which offers to God something to please him, not ourselves: for example, if at Christmas you give a gift to

a friend just to get one for yourself, would this be a gift which is a sacrifice? On the other hand, have you ever given someone a gift just to make that person happy, for example to a small child who can't give you a gift in return? We must be sure that we offer God gifts that cost us something, not money but self-denial, just to please him, to thank him. We should thank God constantly; sacrifice is the best way to do so."

b. "A thanksgiving to God: if a man gave you thousand dollars every month, it would be impolite not to thank him. Yet God gives us so much every day, every minute, yet we might neglect to thank him. We should thank him constantly. Sacrifice is the best way to do so."

c. "Showing sorrow for sin: when you offend someone by an unkind, ugly remark, what should you do?" (Say, "I'm sorry.") "Why? How much more should we tell God, 'I'm sorry' when we offend him. Confession is the best way to do this, and we perform our penance, which is a little sacrifice."

10. *Christ, the perfect priest.* "Let us review what a priest is: one who offers sacrifice in the name of all the people. How is Christ the perfect priest? Remember that to be a good sacrifice it must be offered with a pure heart." (Christ offered with a pure, sinless heart the sacrifice of himself) "What does the name 'Christ' mean?" (the anointed One) "Recall from previous lessons the meaning of 'anointing'." (a symbol of consecration and strength) "When did Christ's 'ordination' take place? Christ became a priest at the moment of his conception, the Incarnation; his divinity is his anointing."

11. Read the acts of Christ the Priest in the Bible: Heb 10:5–7 ("I come"); Mt 26:26–29 (Last Supper); Heb 5:1–10; 7:27.

12. *Melchizedek, a type of Christ.* "How is Melchizedek a type of Christ?" (See Heb 7.) "Turn to p. 51 to appreciate the picture of Melchizedek that is in the cathedral of Chartres. In your missalette find references to Melchizedek. See your text, p. 50, to find out the two places where Christ offered himself."

13. *Christ, perfect Victim.* "What is a victim? Not someone hurt, but a sacrifice that is destroyed. There is no sacrifice without the shedding of blood. *Victima,* in Latin, means a gift involved in a true sacrifice. What does destruction mean? It means that the gift that is so loved is destroyed to show how much we adore, love, and thank God. Read quietly on p. 50 to find out why Christ is the perfect Victim."

14. "Let us review 'reparation'. God is offended; therefore the reparation must be of infinite value. Only God himself can offer a sacrifice of infinite value; therefore the victim must be God. Christ is the perfect Victim."

15. *Mediator.* "The word 'mediator' comes from a Latin word, *medius,* which means "middle." What is a mediator? Turn to p. 51 to find the definition. A mediator is a go-between. How is Christ the true Mediator? Are all priests mediators? Why is Christ the perfect mediator between God and man?" See the chalk talk.

Lesson Plan for a One-day Presentation

1. Pray for priests, as suggested in activity 1.

2. See activities 2–15.

3. Assign p. 20 in the Activity Book.

Suggested Schedule for Five-day Presentation

1. Sacrifice
   Aim: to identify the precise meaning of sacrifice and its relationship to the priesthood.
   Activities: see activities 2 and 3.

2. Old Testament sacrifices
   Aim: to identify and explain a few of the most important Old Testament sacrifices.
   Activities: see activities 4, 5, 6, and 7.

3. Christ the perfect Priest
   Aim: to identify Christ as the fulfillment of the Old Testament priesthood and himself the true Priest.
   Activities: see activities 10, 11, and 12.

4. Christ the perfect Victim
   Aim: to identify Christ as the perfect Victim who alone could expiate the world's sins.
   Activities: see activities 13 and 14.

5. Christ the perfect Mediator
   Aim: to identify Christ as perfect Mediator.
   Activities: see activity 15.

Notes:

CHAPTER 10

Christ, Source of All Grace

Background Reading for the Teachers:

Lawler, pp. 253–262.
Hardon, pp. 172–179.

Aims:

To identify Christ as the source of all grace because of his life, death, and Resurrection; to explain the importance of grace; to give scriptural evidence that Christ is the source of all grace; to understand the ways we receive the grace Christ has won for us and to appreciate the priest's role in this; to understand that we can and should increase grace in our souls.

Materials Needed:

Pen, paper, blackboard, chalk, Bibles, dictionaries.

Activities

1. "The subject of our class today is CHRIST, THE SOURCE OF ALL GRACE." (Have this written on the board.) "How is Christ the source of all grace? See the first paragraph in your text on p. 52. The Son of God became man so that we might receive the gift of God's grace that our first parents lost for us. We call Christ the source of all grace, the One from whom we receive this wonderful gift of God's life in our souls."

2. Put the following analogies on the board. Compare each with the doctrine of Christ as the source of all grace.

Then ask students if they can think of other analogies. Give them a few minutes to write down their ideas.
   a. Christ is the sun.
      We are what is warmed by the sun.
      Grace is the radiation from the sun.
   b. Christ is the vine.
      We are the branches.
      Grace is the life that flows from the vine to the branches.

3. Have the students look up the word "grace" in their dictionaries. Help them to see that, from the origins of the word, it means an *unmerited* favor or gift.

4. Read the third paragraph on p. 52 and prepare to explain the effects of sanctifying grace.

5. *The saints on grace.* "St. Thomas said that one grace is greater than all the treasures in the world. St. Teresa of Avila said that she would die a thousand deaths if only one person might receive the gift of grace. If these saints saw grace as something so precious, you can understand a little better how much Jesus wants us to have it, and why he died so that we might receive it."

6. Assign the following Scripture quotes to single students or groups of students: Jn 1:14–17, 15:4–5; Acts 15:11; Rom 5:1–2, 15, 18–21; Eph 1:15; 2:8–10. Have them look them up and, after deliberation, read them before the class

and explain what they tell us about grace.

7. Read the fifth paragraph on p. 52 to p. 53. Discuss Jesus' supernatural powers over sin and Satan and how that power is shared with his priests as they administer the sacraments.

8. "What are the ways that we receive the grace that Christ has won for us?" Write on board: PRAYER, SACRAMENTS, GOOD WORKS. "Read p. 54 beginning at 'Jesus Gives Grace to All Men'. Whom does God use to give his grace to us?" Write PRIESTS on board. Then underneath write: PRAYERS, PREACHING, ADMINISTERING THE SACRAMENTS. "These are the ways that priests help us to grow in grace."

9. Write the letters GRACE on the board. Have the students memorize the following:

G—GIFT Grace is a gift: God does not owe it to us.

R—REDEMPTION Jesus won grace for us through his redeeming life, death, and Resurrection.

A—ALL All good things come from Christ.

C—CHRIST Christ is the source of all grace.

E—EVERYONE Everyone should try to grow in grace.

Plan for a One-day Presentation

1. Pray the Angelus.

2. See activities 1–9 and the chalk talk above.

3. Assign p. 21 in the Activity Book.

Notes:

Suggested Schedule for a Five-day Presentation:

1. Grace and Christ, the source of grace

   Aim: to identify Christ as the source of grace.
   Activities: see activities 1, 2, and 3.

2. The importance of grace
   Aim: to identify Christ's special powers as signs of his divine mission.
   Activities: See activities 4 and 5.

3. Scriptural evidence for Christ as the source of all grace
   Aim: continuation of above.
   Activities: see activities 6 and 7.

4. Jesus gives grace to all men
   Aim: to identify the new life of grace Christ has won for all, and priests' role as "other Christs".
   Activities: see activities 8, 9, and the chalk talk.

5. Review day
   Aim: to summarize material.
   Activity: test.

CHAPTER 11

Jesus Founds His Church

Background Reading for the Teacher:

Lawler, pp. 174–194.
Hardon, pp. 206–223.

Aims:

To foster faith in the authority of the Church; to locate and explain the meaning of the calling of the twelve apostles; to identify and prove that Peter is head of the Church; to perceive how the apostles share the authority of Jesus Christ; to identify and explain various images of the Church; and to list and explain the four marks of the Church.

Materials Needed:

Pen, paper, Bibles, texts, blackboard, chalk, small rock, keys, tape; optional: costumes, Catholic periodicals, filmstrip projector, filmstrips, poster paper, scissors, colored pens, basin, water, towels.

Activities

1. Pray the Act of Faith on p. 167. "We prayed the Act of Faith because faith enables us to see that Christ is truly present in the Holy Catholic Church; we need this faith to understand how the Pope and the bishops speak in the name of Christ."

2. *Call of the apostles.* "Let us read together the section on p. 55 'Jesus Calls the Twelve Apostles'." Ask:
   a. "Who are the Twelve?" (the foundation members of the new people of God, the Church)
   b. "Why twelve?" (The choice of the Twelve reminded them that Christ's Church was a continuation of God's Chosen People, who were composed of twelve tribes, descendants of the twelve sons of Jacob.)

Talk about the need for "charter members". "Let us pretend that you are starting a new club: the 'Motorcycle Club' or the 'Fun Club', for example. What are some of the things you must do to have a successful club?" Some possible answers are:

a. You must have an aim.
b. You must have a leader.

c. You must have some charter members, like a "board of directors" who will help the leader direct the club.

d. You must recruit new members.

"Now Jesus was starting the Catholic Church. His aim was to save people and lead them to his Father. Christ himself was the leader, but because he would be returning to heaven at the end of his earthly life and would be directing the Church from heaven, he chose Peter to be his visible head on earth. For 'charter memberships' he chose the twelve apostles, who would seek out new members, their converts."

3. Read in the Bible about the twelve apostles.

   a. *The calls* (Jn 1:35–51; Mk 1:16–20; Lk 5:24–28). "We see in these readings how Christ called the Twelve; frequently one apostle brought another to Jesus; the call, the vocation to the priesthood is a mystery of God's choice."

   b. *The need for the apostles.* (Mt 9:35–38). "Jesus is our Good Shepherd. When he saw all the people so sad and confused, he felt sorry for them; he called laborers to 'harvest' them."

4. Write on the board: *Ubi Petrus ibi ecclesia.* "Does anyone know what these words mean?" ("Where Peter is, there is the Church!") "Why? Let us read together in the text beginning with the last paragraph on p. 55." Ask:

   a. "Why did Jesus choose Simon?" (to give his Church a supreme leader, one who would be his own representative on earth)

   b. "Why did Jesus change Simon's name to Peter?" (To signify that Simon Peter had a new mission. Peter [Cephas] means rock.)

   c. "What truth did the apostles, the early Christians, and the whole Church teach from then on?" (that Peter and each of his successors are the visible head of the Church on earth)

5. "Memorize Mt 16:16–19. What does it say? Turn to p. 56. What does it mean?" (that Peter is the supreme and visible head of the Church on earth) *Peter's "key"*. "What is a key?" (Discuss the comparison of our notion of key to the notion of key as a sign of power; relate it to the power of the Pope.) Show a key. "A key can open and close. The Pope has the keys to the Kingdom of Heaven. What does that mean?"

   Hold up a rock. Discuss rock as a symbol of strength. (rock of faith, rock on which Church is built, which can withstand storms)

   Binding and loosing. Take some tape and bind up something, then loosen it. Compare this to the power of the Pope to bind and loose.

6. "What spiritual gifts did Jesus give to the apostles, his first bishops? Turn to pp. 56–57 for the answer. Recall what we learned about the saving mission of Jesus in lesson 8. What is it?" (to teach, rule, sanctify) "How did the apostles share in this mission? Make a chart showing (1) their mission, and (2) scriptural proof of this sharing."

   "Memorize Lk 10:16 and Jn 20:23." Explain the meaning of these essential passages.

7. "Jesus made the apostles shepherds. What does that mean? Why does the image of a shepherd very well describe the role of the apostles?" Read Jn 10:11, Lk 15:3–17; Mt 6:34.

8. Have a prayer project for the spiritual support of the bishop. Pray daily for your bishop by name. Have a chart

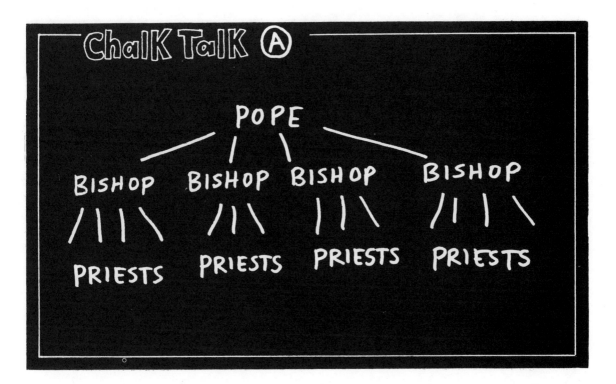

showing different spiritual exercises (Mass, Rosary, visit to the Blessed Sacrament, etc.) Post the chart so that the students can sign up to assure they will pray for their bishop.

9. See chalk talk A on the hierarchy.

10. See chalk talk B on the Communion of Saints.

11. *Jesus, the ideal teacher*. "Jesus used images that would help the people to understand his spiritual message. Please read pp. 57–58 on 'The Church of Jesus Christ'. Every time you read about an image of the Church, list it; then be ready to explain the meaning of this image." Prepare a chart showing the image of the Church. Complete the project by writing or illustrating the messages.

Image	Meaning	Reference
Sheepfold	We are the sheep cared for by our shepherd	Jn. 10:1–18

12. Discuss marks, proofs of authenticity. "Can a real diamond be identified? How?" (By its power to cut glass; an imitation stone cannot do this.) "In former times a king would place his seal on official documents. Why?" (to certify that the message was authentic) "There are marks of the Church. Because God wanted us to be certain of the authenticity of a message claimed to be his, he gave his Church four marks. Turn to p. 58 in your textbook. What are these marks and what does each signify?"

13. Use pp. 22–23 of the Activity Book as a review of this chapter.

Lesson Plan for a One-day Presentation

1. Pray the Act of Faith (see activity 1, above).

2. See activities 2–12.

3. Assign pp. 22–23 in the Activity Book.

Suggested Schedule for a Five-day Presentation

1. The new Chosen People of God; the call of the twelve apostles
   Aim: to foster faith in Church authority; to identify the new Chosen People of God as the Catholic Church; to locate and to explain the meaning of the apostles' calling; to describe the qualities of a true apostle of Jesus Christ.
   Activities: see activity 2.

2. The new Chosen People of God; the call of the twelve apostles

Aim: see day 1.
Activities: see activity 3.

3. Simon Peter, head of the Church
   Aim: to identify Peter as the first visible head of the Church; to discuss the powers of the Pope.
   Activities: see activities 4 and 5.

4. The first bishops and their special powers
   Aim: to perceive how the apostles share the authority of Christ.
   Activities: see activities 6, 7, 8, 9, and 10.

5. Images of the Church; the four marks of the Church
   Aim: to identify the images of the Church; to prove that the Church can be identified as the true Church by her four marks.
   Activities: see activities 11 and 12.
   Review: see activity 13.

CHAPTER 12

The Church in Our Time

Background Reading for the Teacher:

Lawler, pp. 194–221.
Hardon, pp. 224–238.

Aims:

To identify the birthday of the Church; to explain that the Holy Spirit is the soul of the Church; to describe the spread of the early Church; to define infallibility and indefectibility; to distinguish what can change from what cannot change in the Church.

Materials Needed:

Texts, paper, pen, blackboard, Bibles; optional: map, poster paper, pen (colored), wadded paper (orange).

Activities

1. Pray the Apostles' Creed on p. 167. Remind the students that this Creed came from the twelve apostles.

2. "When was the last time you went to a birthday party? Did you have fun? Why are birthdays so special? Today we are going to think about a birthday, a very important birthday; the birthday of the Catholic Church. Does anyone know the date?"

   Have a dramatization. Select one girl to be Mary. Place her in the middle of twelve boys, and some other girls and boys. Direct them to look as if they are praying. Have someone from the back of the room make a noise "like a strong, driving wind". Have someone else throw small wads of orange-colored paper, which look like tongues of fire.

3. "Please turn to p. 68. What do you see? The name of the picture is 'The Seven Joys of Mary' by Memling. What is Mary doing?" (praying) "Who is above her?" (the Holy Spirit) "Who are surrounding her?" (the apostles) "Why are their hands raised?" (to receive the gifts of the Holy Spirit)

4. Compare the Holy Spirit in the Church to a soul in a human body. "Let us review the meaning of the human person. Man equals body and _____. If he

does not have a soul, is he alive? Remember that Adam became a true man when God breathed into him a soul. Now, as we learned in our last lesson, the Church is the Mystical Body of Christ. As a true mystical body, the Church must have both a _____ and a _____. The body is seen in her visible members, her outward structure, such as the disciples of Christ in the upper room. But the body does not become animated, alive, until there is a soul. That soul is the _____ (Holy Spirit)."

"The soul directs the body and tells it what to do. For example, you told yourself to get up this morning, go to school, and be good in class. Likewise, the Holy Spirit, the soul of the Church, directs its members, the body, to do great things for God. For example, right after the Holy Spirit descended upon the apostles, how many people were converted by the apostles? The answer is in your text. The Holy Spirit is like an invisible electrical current, swiftly moving and energizing. List all the activities that happened in the early Church because of the Holy Spirit. You can find answers on p. 61."

5. Read the section "The Church Spreads throughout the World." Make a diagram showing the places to which the apostles went. Hold up to your students a map of the ancient times. Point out to them the various places mentioned in the text: Rome, Greece, Russia, Spain, Jerusalem, Asia Minor, Armenia, India, Palestine, Iran, Ethiopia, Turkey.

6. Write INFALLIBILITY on the board. "Does anyone know what this word means? Let us try to make a logical guess. *In* in Latin means 'not'; *fallere* in Latin means 'to err'. So, infallibility means the ability not to err. Turn to the section 'The Spirit's Gifts to the Church' on p. 62. What does your book say infallibility is? Do we have any scriptural basis for this? Jesus promised us that he would send us the Holy Spirit of Truth, who would instruct his apostles in everything (Jn 16:16–17). This means that the Spirit of Truth guides the Pope and the bishops united with the Pope. Please open your Bibles to Mt 28:20. What does the Bible say?" ("I will be with you always.") "How does this passage relate to infallibility? It relates to infallibility because, if the Pope and bishops can make a mistake in proposing for our belief matters in faith and morals, then Jesus is not truly with them, for Jesus cannot make a mistake. Now, you know infallibility does not mean the Pope is perfect in his personal life. Some people get this confused with infallibility. No, the Pope's infallibility means he cannot make a mistake when teaching on faith and morals, although he can certainly sin and make mistakes in his personal life."

"To remember infallibility, remember that falling means to go down. The Church will never fall down and make a mistake."

7. Write INDEFECTIBILITY on the board. "What does 'defective' mean? Don't you think of something imperfect, something that is ruined or is not complete, such as a defective watch? Indefectibility is a *perfection* of the Church: the Church will be present on earth until the end of the world. One definition of "defector" is one who leaves a cause. The Church will never abandon her cause of bringing men to salvation, as Jesus promised (Mt 16:18). He said that not even the powers of hell, with all their force, would prevail over his Church. And our Catholic Church has

remained on earth from its very beginning at the day of Pentecost. Indefectibility means not only that the Church will remain here, visibly present, but that her mission will remain. Let us read about this indefectibility in the last paragraph of p. 62."

To remember indefectibility, remember that defect means to leave. The Church will never leave the world or her sacred mission."

8. "What can change in the Church? What can never change? Look to p. 63 for answers. Some examples of things that do not change are the divinity of Christ, the papacy, the sacraments, imitation of Christ's virtues, and worship of God in prayer. Some examples of things that do change or have changed are certain rituals of the Mass, such as the priest facing the people instead of the altar; the language of the Mass; and Mass for Sunday offered on Saturday night.

Lesson Plan for a One-day Presentation

1. Pray the Apostles' Creed on page 167; see activity 1.

Notes:

2. See activities 1–8.

3. Assign p. 24 in the Activity Book.

Suggested Schedule for a Five-day Presentation

1. Pentecost, the birthday of the Church
   Aim: to identify the birthday of the Church; to explain how the Holy Spirit is the soul of the Church.
   Activities: see activities 2, 3, 4, and 5.

2. The Church spreads throughout the world
   Aim: to describe the spread of the early Church and what this spread means.
   Activities: see activity 5.

3. Infallibility and indefectibility
   Aim: to define and explain these two terms.
   Activities: see activities 6 and 7.

4. Infallibility and indefectibility
   Aim: see day 3.
   Activities: see activities 6 and 7.

5. Mission of the Church
   Aim: to review the precise mission of the Church and to discern what can change and what cannot change.
   Activities: see activity 8.

PART THREE

God Shares His Life

CHAPTER 13

Doctrine of Grace

Background Reading for the Teacher:

Lawler, pp. 360–370.
Hardon, pp. 172–193.
See Special Material for the Teacher, below.

Aims:

To review the definition of grace; to define actual grace and exemplify its uses; to identify, define, and explain the meaning and importance of sanctifying grace; to clarify the three kinds of life (plant, animal, human) in order to explain that grace elevates us above the natural human life to supernatural life; and to distinguish between natural and supernatural life.

Materials Needed:

Pen, paper, blackboard.

Special Material for the Teacher

I. The Importance, Dignity, and Excellence of Grace

The teaching of the doctrine on grace demands a clear perception from you, the catechist, for this doctrine represents the most practically important teaching in our faith: the working out of our salvation and sanctification. The doctrine on grace is often omitted in catechisms operating from a materialistic, modernistic philosophy, which reduces religion to mere psychologism. This omission neglects to portray grace as a real dimension in the believer, radically transforming him into a "new man in Christ". Thus, these particular sections on grace are vitally important for you to teach, since grace makes up the inner life of the Church and of the individual believer. You as a catechist must be convinced of its volitional and intellectual significance.

Volitionally, this doctrine can show that "ineffable supernatural life which animates and sustains the Church, and which, in spite of the malice and sloth of men, the hostility from without, and indolence, inertia and sluggishness within, gives the Church an imperishable and autonomous existence and fills it with an indescribable charm."[1] The beauty and splendor of the supernatural, prayerfully taught, can attract our students and move their wills to embrace the truth they perceive.

Intellectually, our students must know with utmost clarity that they can be saved only by remaining in the state of grace. They must look upon grace as a source from which all good works flow and to which they must keep returning in order to persevere and grow in virtue. Without grace, we are dead. With grace, we are alive, able to cooperate with God who will fructify us and bring us into heavenly glory.

II. The Precise Definition of Grace

Precisely, what is grace? Grace is a supernatural gift, which God of his free benevolence bestows on rational creatures for their eternal salvation.[2] Grace can be considered in three ways: *uncreated grace*, which refers to God himself, inasmuch as he indwells the justified; *created grace*, man's specific sharing in the life of God himself; and *actual grace*, a transient help of God enlightening the mind and strengthening the will to do good and to avoid evil.

Grace, as has been stated, is entirely supernatural, that is, above nature. Grace does not come from man's natural powers; thus, it is entirely gratuitous. These points are important, insofar as heresies have risen due to misconceptions on these doctrines. For example, Pelagianism regarded grace as within man's natural capacity; semi-Pelagianism, although not relegating grace entirely to free will, taught that man's primary desire comes from his natural powers and that he does not need grace to persevere in virtue.

On the other hand, the Protestant reformers entirely denied man's free will and his ability to cooperate with grace. Today, modern rationalism denies the supernatural; this rationalism poses as a contemporary Pelagianism. Thus, as a teacher, you must make these points clear to your students, so they will not fall into error.

III. Sanctifying Grace

Sanctifying grace is a supernatural state of being infused by God, which permanently inheres in the soul. This grace is a real participation in the divine nature (cf. 2 Pet 1:4; Jn 1:12, 18; 3:5; 1 Jn 3; 1 Pet 1:23). Its supernatural assimilation to God is completed in heaven by the beatific vision. Grace, the seed of glory, is destined to blossom perfectly in heaven.

Having defined sanctifying grace, we should examine its effects. This habitual grace sanctifies the soul, that is, the soul is free from mortal sin and is permanently attentive to God. It also gives a supernatural beauty to the soul. In the words of the *Roman Catechism*, "Grace is . . ., as it were, a certain brilliance or light which cleanses all stains from our souls and makes them more beautiful and more brilliant."[3] Sanctifying grace makes one a friend and child of God, and an heir to heaven. Through sanctifying grace, man becomes a real temple of the Holy Spirit.

A Catholic's primary duty is both to retain and to develop this relationship with God, a relationship caused by sanctifying grace. Only in the state of grace can one merit further graces and heaven. It is a mortal sin, moreover, to receive any of the "sacraments of the living" if one is not in the state of grace. (In these times of few confessions and numerous Communions, it is important to stress this point with your stu-

[1] John G. Arintero, *The Mystical Evolution* (Rockford, Il.: Tan Books, 1978), p. 3.

[2] Ludwig Ott, *Fundamentals of Catholic Dogma* (Rockford, Il.: Tan Books, 1974), p. 220.

[3] *The Roman Catechism,* as quoted in ibid., p. 257.

dents.) Only those who die in God's grace can enter his Kingdom. One deliberate mortal sin can lose all former graces.

IV. Actual Grace

Actual grace is a temporary supernatural act of God directed toward man for the purpose of moving him to do a good act.[4] This grace internally and directly enlightens the intellect and strengthens the will. Why is actual grace necessary? The Church teaches as *de fide* that "for every salutary act internal supernatural grace of God is absolutely necessary". It is essential for the beginning of faith and salvation, for the performance of salutary acts, for final perseverance, and for the avoiding of all venial sins.

This grace, furthermore, cannot be merited by natural works, petitions of a purely natural prayer, or man's dispositions. God

wills all men to be saved; thus, it can be understood that he gives all sufficient grace to observe his commandments, enough grace for conversions, and the adequate graces necessary for innocent unbelievers to achieve eternal salvation.

Activities

1. "Pray the Hail Mary. How did we address Mary in this prayer? This title of 'full of grace' relates to our lesson, which is all about grace. What is grace?" (Write GRACE on the board.) "Please turn to p. 67 to find the answer. Grace is a supernatural gift from God given to us through Jesus Christ."

2. Review Activity 10 from Chapter 10.

3. "There are three things we must—and the word is MUST—do in this life:
   a. We must persevere in the state of grace.

---

[4] Ibid., 225.

b. If we do fall into mortal sin, we must quickly get out of this state.

c. We must grow daily in grace."

See chalk talk A.

"Now it is very hard to do these things: we are easily tempted into sin, we stay in sin, and we get lazy. That is why God gives us actual grace: we persevere by prayers and good works in our state of grace; we repent if we are in mortal sin; and we continue to respond to all the graces God gives and to grow in grace.

4. Chalk talk B on "Different Kinds of Life."

5. "Why is grace called supernatural? Read the third paragraph on p. 67. Grace is called supernatural because it is above our natural powers. *Super* is Latin for 'above'. If a horse spoke, laughed, and debated, we would say the horse had supernatural powers. Why? So, when man becomes very close to God, so close that he is called a child of God, we say it is truly supernatural, above man's natural condition."

6. Supernatural or natural? (This can be read or copies can be made and distributed. Write N for natural, S for supernatural, and N & S for those things that might be both.)

a._____ Seeing the beauty of the Grand Canyon

b._____ Watching T.V. on Saturday morning

c._____ Saying a Rosary

d._____ Going for a swim

e._____ Going to a party

f._____ Getting married

g._____ Becoming a sister

h._____ Receiving Jesus in Holy Communion

i.＿＿ Caring for a sick stranger out of love for Jesus

j.＿＿ Helping your best friend when he or she is in trouble

7. Compare sanctifying grace to a telescope. "Sanctifying grace is like a telescope. How? What does a telescope do? Sanctifying grace is like a telescope because it helps us see with the eyes of faith things we could not normally see, such as God's love for us, God's beauty, Jesus' Presence in the Eucharist, Mary's maternal love, the reality of our guardian angels, etc. We do not see physically, but with the eyes of faith. Grace enables us, like a telescope, to see things we cannot see with our own human vision."

8. Discuss actual grace. "God gives us not only sanctifying grace, but also 'temporary' helps, 'lifts' that keep us good. What are they called? These graces are called ACTUAL GRACES." (Write this on the board.) "What are some examples of actual grace? What examples are given in the book on p. 68? Other examples of actual graces are: making a visit to the Blessed Sacrament; saying devoutly the names of Jesus and Mary; offering to visit someone who is lonely; smiling at and being nice to someone in your class who feels left out; giving up something you like to eat as a sacrifice to God; offering up little pains in reparation for sin; offering to help your mother with the dishes before she asks you."

9. "Make a list of actual graces all through the day. You may look in your religion text: there are many occasions of actual grace in it. Actual graces often change lives. For example, St. Francis Borgia was not very devout. One day he saw a corpse, the body of the Empress Isabella, who had just died. Empress Isabella had been a very beautiful young queen. When he saw how ugly she looked he realized how short life is and how silly it is to prize earthly things above spiritual things. Seeing a dead body for this saint was a great actual grace."

10. List the following situations on slips of paper. Then play charades. Divide the class into two teams. Representatives of both teams take turns picking the slips. They (and however many more team members are needed) silently act out for their own teams the situations described. Their own team must guess what action is being portrayed and say whether it is an example of an actual grace or a sanctifying grace. If the team members guess correctly, the team receives a point.

   a. Two people are arguing. They are getting more and more angry. One gets so angry that he looks as if he is going to hit the other. All of the sudden he calms down, smiles, and offers his hand to the other in friendship. (actual)

   b. A baby is getting baptized. (sanctifying)

   c. A boy breaks a window. The father comes into the room and sees it. He calls the family members together and questions them. The boy hesitates a minute but then comes forward and confesses. (actual)

   d. Someone is receiving Communion. (sanctifying)

   e. Someone is shopping in a store. She looks furtively around; then she starts to put something in her purse. She hesitates and then puts it back on the shelf. (actual)

   f. Someone in bed is being anointed by a priest. (sanctifying)

81

g. Someone is taking care of an old, irritable person cheerfully. (actual)

h. Someone is going to confession. (sanctifying)

i. Two people are getting married. (sanctifying)

j. Someone in a hurry passes a blind person and helps him to get across the street. (actual)

Lesson Plan for a One-day Presentation

1. Pray the Hail Mary, as suggested in activity 1, above.

2. See activities 2–10.

3. Assign p. 25 in the Activity Book.

Suggested Schedule for a Five-day Presentation

1. What is grace?
   Aim: to explain both the need for and the meaning of grace.
   Activities: see activities 1, 2, and 3.

2. The meaning and importance of actual grace
   Aim: to define actual grace and exemplify its uses.
   Activities: see activities 8, 9, and 10.

3. The meaning and importance of sanctifying grace
   Aim: to identify, define, and explain the meaning and importance of sanctifying grace.
   Activities: see activities 7 and 10.

4. Kinds of life
   Aim: to clarify the three kinds of life (plant, animal, human) in order to explain that grace elevates us above the natural human life to supernatural life; to distinguish between natural and supernatural life.
   Activities: see activities 4, 5, and 6.

5. Review
   Aim: to summarize the doctrine on grace and its importance in our lives.
   Activities: play a review game or use other review methods.

Notes:

CHAPTER 14

Faith, Hope, and Charity

Background Reading for the Teacher:

Lawler, pp. 282–298.
Hardon, pp. 193–197.
See Special Material for the Teacher, below.

Aims:

To identify and explain the meaning of virtue; to distinguish between natural and supernatural virtue; to identify the three supernatural virtues—faith, hope, and charity; to define, explain, and give examples of faith, hope, and charity.

Materials Needed:

Blackboard, copies of exercise (activity 4), paper, colored markers, pictures of Mother Teresa (optional).

Special Material for the Teacher

I. Infused Virtues

An infused virtue is a virtue "poured forth" by God so that we can cooperate with sanctifying grace and can perform supernatural actions to achieve a supernatural end. When sanctifying grace is poured into us, God "channels" this life into specific supernatural habits, namely, the theological and cardinal virtues. It is important to note that God literally pours in (*infundere*) these virtues without our assistance. For example, baptized infants have all the supernatural virtues. All these virtues, except faith and hope, are lost by one mortal sin. Faith can be lost only by a mortal sin against faith, and hope is lost only by a mortal sin against hope.[1]

II. Theological Virtues

The three virtues of faith, hope, and charity are called "theological virtues" (*Theos* is a Greek word meaning "God") insofar as they have God as their immediate object. These virtues specifically direct us to our final end, God. They not only help us go out to, but also to reach, God, by empowering us to know (faith), desire (hope), and

[1] Edward J. Gratsch, S.T.D., ed., *Principles of Catholic Theology* (New York: Alba House, 1981), p. 269.

83

love (charity) him. Unlike other virtues, there is no "golden mean", or "happy medium", connected with faith, hope, and charity. We can never believe, hope in, and love God too much!

III. Moral Virtues

The moral virtues are concerned with the *means* by which we achieve our supernatural destiny. They are supernatural habits that build upon our natural prudence, justice, fortitude, and temperance.

First of all, what are the four natural moral virtues? The four natural moral virtues, or cardinal virtues, correspond to the four faculties of the soul: intellect, will, the appetite of desire, and the appetite of aversion. Prudence disciplines the intellect, justice the will, temperance the desire for pleasure, and fortitude the aversion to the painful.

Because sanctifying grace empowers us to act beyond our natural capacities, it is fitting that there exist supernatural moral virtues, inclining to supernatural moral ends our four faculties of the intellect, will, desire for pleasure, and aversion toward the painful. In our society, there is a distinct tendency to understress the supernatural moral virtues, in favor of the more natural virtues associated with activism and horizontalism. Thus, it is important not only to teach clearly the superiority of the supernatural virtues, but also to inspire and direct your students to cooperate with the many gifts of grace they have as healthy (or potentially healthy) members of the Catholic Church.

Activities

1. Have the students look up the definition of virtue in dictionaries. Discuss the definition.

2. Give the Latin derivative of virtue, *virtus,* which means "strength". In chalk talk A, discuss the need for exercising the virtues.

3. Read the second paragraph on p. 69 and discuss the difference between natural and supernatural virtue.

4. To explain natural and supernatural virtues write the following on the chalk board:

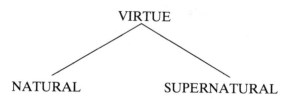

Give the students this exercise, having them write N for natural and S for supernatural:

a.____ Denying oneself food so as to make a sacrifice out of love for Jesus.

b.____ Denying oneself food so as to have an attractive figure or physique.

c.____ Helping others in order to imitate Jesus' love for them.

d.____ Helping others because they will owe us a favor.

e.____ Spreading devotion to Mary.

f.____ Making visits to the Blessed Sacrament.

g.____ Controlling one's tongue so as not to get into trouble.

h.____ Controlling one's tongue so as to imitate the meekness of Jesus.

i.____ Studying hard so as to get all A's.

j.____ Studying hard so as to fulfill one's obligations as a student.

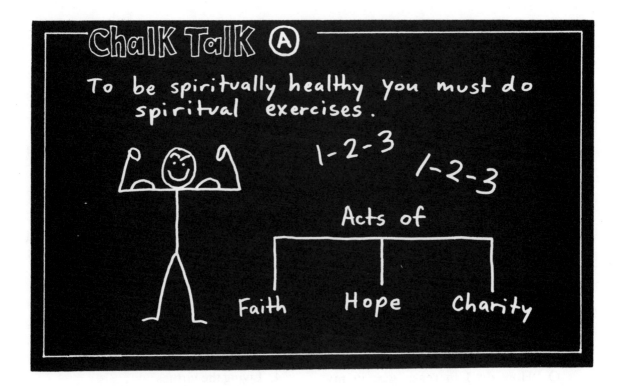

Chalk Talk Ⓐ

To be spiritually healthy you must do spiritual exercises.

1-2-3 1-2-3

Acts of

Faith   Hope   Charity

5. Continue the diagram from activity 4, adding:

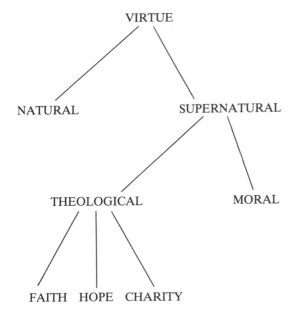

VIRTUE

NATURAL   SUPERNATURAL

THEOLOGICAL   MORAL

FAITH   HOPE   CHARITY

6. Read the sections on faith, hope, and charity on pp. 69–71. Discuss the definition of each.

7. Make a chart showing how three saints practiced the virtue of faith.

8. Make a chart showing how three saints practiced the virtue of hope.

9. Make a chart showing how three saints practiced the virtue of charity.

10. Tell the story of Mother Teresa of Calcutta and how she witnesses to the love of God and to love of neighbor for the love of God. Show pictures, if possible.

11. After you are quite sure the students understand the theological virtues, have three students play at being personifications of faith, hope, and charity. (Put tags on them to identify each of them.) Interview them with the ques-

tions below. Have the remaining students critique their answers.

Q. "If I don't believe in God, which of you am I lacking?"

Q. "If I get too discouraged by my problems and think that there is no solution, which of you am I lacking?"

Q. "If I am unkind to others, which of you am I lacking?"

Q. "If I think that I am so bad that God cannot help me, which of you am I lacking?"

Q. "Every time I sin, which of you am I lacking?"

Q. "If I were to commit a mortal sin, which of you would I lose completely?"

Q. "Will you have an end and if so when?"

Q. "Which of you is the greatest and why?"

Q. "How do I increase you in my soul?"

Lesson Plan for a One-day Presentation

1. Pray the Acts of Faith, Hope, and Love (charity) (pp. 167–168).

2. See activities 1–11, above.

3. Assign pp. 26–27 in the Activity Book.

Suggested Schedule for a Five-day Presentation

1. Virtue
   Aim: to explain the meaning of virtue and the difference between supernatural and natural virtue.
   Activities: see activities 1, 2, 3, and 4.

2. Theological virtues
   Aim: to identify the three theological virtues and explain and give the meaning of each.
   Activities: see activities 5 and 6.

3. Living the virtues
   Aim: to give examples of how one lives and practices the theological virtues.
   Activities: see activities 7, 8, 9, and 10.

4. Living the virtues
   Aim: see day 3.
   Activities: see activities 5 and 6.

5. Review
   Aim: to summarize the points of the lesson.
   Activity: see activity 11.

Notes:

CHAPTER 15

The Cardinal Virtues

Background Reading for the Teacher:

Lawler, pp. 299–301.
Hardon, pp. 197–209.

Aims:

To explain the difference between the theological and the cardinal virtues; to explain and exemplify the virtues of prudence, justice, temperance, and fortitude; and to memorize the definitions of the moral virtues and the eight Beatitudes.

Materials Needed:

Pen, paper, blackboard, poster paper, rulers, colored pens.

Activities

1. Pray, using some of the petitions from the Litany of the Blessed Virgin Mary on p. 169, such as: "Mother most chaste, pray for us" . . . ; "Virgin most prudent" . . . ; "Mirror of Justice" . . . ; or "Tower of David". Explain how each of these titles shows how our Lady possessed the moral virtues of temperance, prudence, justice, and fortitude.

2. Read the first three paragraphs on p. 74. Put this diagram on the board (first part is a review of previous chapter).

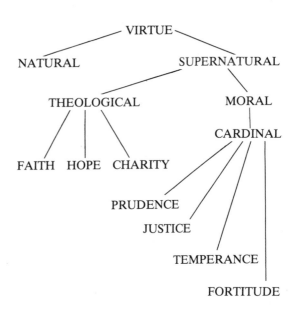

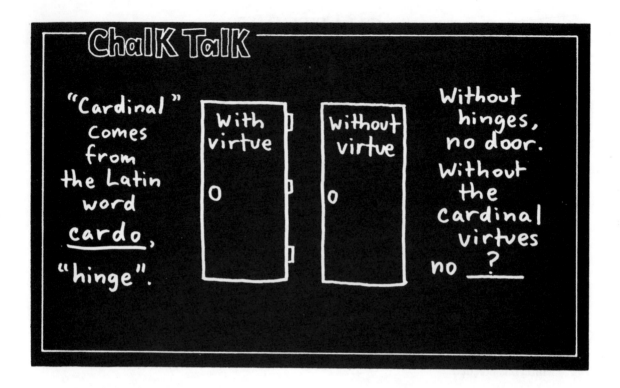

ChalK TalK

"Cardinal" comes from the Latin word cardo, "hinge".

With virtue

Without virtue

Without hinges, no door. Without the cardinal virtues no ___?___

3. Give a chalk talk on the meaning of the cardinal virtues.

4. After reading the sections on the four virtues on pp. 74 and 75, show the difference between the natural and the supernatural virtues through examples:

prudence (natural prudence indicates the best way to earn money, whereas supernatural prudence indicates the best way to get to heaven and to help others to get there);

justice (paying taxes vs. teaching the faith to children);

temperance (dieting so as not to gain weight vs. giving up some food for a penance); and

fortitude (athletic training vs. suffering martyrdom).

5. Bring in several accounts of the saints or holy people. Assign students to look up and report on saints who exemplified the four cardinal virtues and how they did so. Below are some possibilities.

prudence: St. Ignatius of Loyola, St. Francis de Sales, St. Philip Neri, St. Teresa of Avila (all had great prudence with regard to counseling souls);

temperance: Matt Talbot (an alcoholic who overcame his intemperance and became a very holy man), St. Camillus de Lellis (overcame a serious problem with gambling);

fortitude: St. Maximilian Kolbe, Bl. Margaret Clitherow, St. Titus Brandsma, St. Ursula and her companions, any other martyr;

justice: St. Thomas More, St. Louis IX.

6. After you are sure that the students understand the cardinal virtues, have four

students personify the virtues. Make signs to identify each one for the rest of the students. Interview them and have the other students critique their answers.

Q. "Why are you called cardinal virtues?"

Q. "Which of you is the ability to make right choices?"

Q. "Which of you is the power of self-control?"

Q. "Which of you helps us to give to everyone what he deserves?"

Q. "Which of you is the ability to face difficulty and danger with courage?"

Q. "If I decide not to stay up really late so that at school I will not be sleepy and unable to concentrate, which virtue am I using?"

Q. "If I go to the aid of someone who is being bullied even though the bully is bigger and stronger than I am, which virtue am I using?"

Q. "If I resist eating that second piece of cake that will make me feel sick, which virtue am I using?"

Q. "If I give a younger brother or sister a fair amount of money for helping me clean my room, which virtue am I using?"

Q. "If I spend too much time watching T.V., which virtue am I lacking?"

Q. "If I bully my brothers and sisters so that I get more than my share of things, which virtues am I lacking?"

Q. "If I often do silly things that cause trouble to myself or others, which virtue am I lacking?"

Q. "If I am overly afraid of getting hurt, which virtue am I lacking?"

Q. "What sort of things should we do to increase you in us?"

(prudence: pray, try to think before you act, think of what Jesus would do; temperance: pray, give up something that is all right for you to have. In this way, you can strengthen your will to resist too much of anything; fortitude: pray, try doing things that are hard for you because they frighten you; justice: pray, think of how you would like others to treat you and treat them that way.)

Q. "Does practicing you make us happier or sadder and why?"

7. Memorize the four cardinal virtues with their definitions; also memorize the eight Beatitudes.

Lesson Plan for a One-day Presentation

1. Pray, using some of the petitions from the Litany of the Blessed Virgin Mary in activity 1, above.

2. See activities 2–7.

3. Assign pp. 28–29 in the Activity Book.

Suggested Schedule for a Five-day Presentation

1. The meaning of the cardinal virtues
   Aim: to explain the purpose of the cardinal virtues and to distinguish these virtues from the theological virtues.
   Activities: see activities 2 and 3.

2. The cardinal virtues
   Aim: to explain and exemplify the cardinal virtues.
   Activities: see activity 4.

3. Identifying the virtues
   Aim: to identify the moral virtues and to see examples of them in the lives of the saints.
   Activities: see activity 5.

4. Living the virtues
   Aim: to be able to practice the virtues in our everyday lives.
   Activities: see activity 6.

5. Review

CHAPTER 16

The Seven Sacraments

Background Reading for the Teacher:

Lawler, pp. 399—408.

Hardon, pp. 504—505.

Aims:

To identify and explain the meaning of sacraments; to explain the notion of "sign"; to identify the sacraments as "signs of Christ"; to identify and explain the matter and form of sacraments; and to identify and exemplify the sacramental grace of each sacrament.

Materials Needed:

Pen, paper, blackboard, text, statue of Mary, missalettes.

Activities

1. Write SACRAMENT on the board. Explain its etymology. "Sacrament comes from the Latin *sacra,* which means 'holy'. Why?" (Sacraments are holy.) "Also, sacrament comes from the Latin word for the Greek *mysterion.* Why? *Mysterion* refers to the mystery of God in Christ in which St. Paul sees God's plan unfolding among men (Col 1:26). Through the sacraments, we encounter the mysterious action of God with us. Do you ever wonder 'What is life all about?' or 'Where can I find Christ today?' We directly encounter Christ in the sacraments."

2. Describe the sacraments as the living waters of grace. "The sacraments are like fountains from which flow gushing waters, life-giving waters of grace. Let us see what the Scriptures say about this grace." Direct students to look up passages and read aloud the following references: Is 12:49; Jn 4:14; 7:37–38; 10:10; 1 Jn 5:8; Rev 22:1–2. "Sketch a design or picture showing how sacraments are living waters of grace."

3. "Think of signs in everyday life. I will give you one minute to think and then we will see what you come up with. Look for signs in our classroom. Why are they signs? To what extent do we

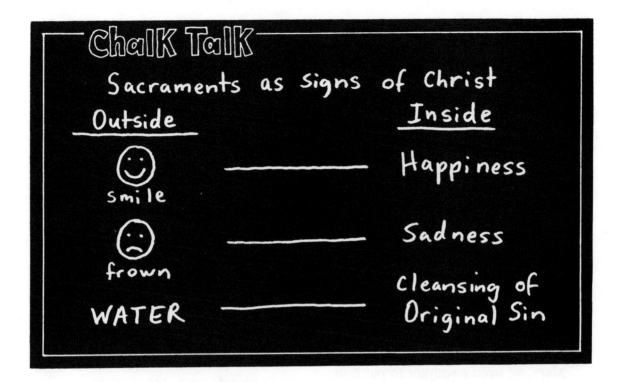

Chalk Talk

Sacraments as Signs of Christ

Outside   Inside

☺ ———————— Happiness
smile

☹ ———————— Sadness
frown

WATER ———————— Cleansing of Original Sin

rely on signs? For example, when we talk with each other? Read in your book, on p. 81, the section 'What Is a Sacrament?' There is a very big difference between daily signs and the signs of the sacraments. Read the section 'The Signs of the Sacraments' on pp. 81–82. What is this difference?"

4. Have a chalk talk about "Sacraments as Signs of Christ". After explaining how sacraments are outward signs of inner grace, ask the students to fill in the chart on the board by listing sacraments and showing what they are signs of.

5. "Take out missalettes and Bibles. We are going to see how often Christ points to signs. Open your Activity Books to p. 30. I will give you twenty minutes to complete this assignment. You will have to look up the prayers in your missalettes."

6. Discuss matter and form.
a. "Every sacrament has matter and form. What does this mean? Well, let us look to matter and form in other things, for example, this statue of Mary. The matter of anything is its material makeup. What is the material in this statue?" (the wood, plaster, etc.) "The form of anything is what makes the material to be something specific. What makes the plaster of this statue to be the likeness of Mary?" (the shape and features of Mary) "Let us look at a cake. What are the material ingredients in a cake?" (flour, sugar, eggs) "What is the formal part of the cake?" (the recipe, because it brings the material ingredients together in such a way as to form a specific food, a cake)

"Now we can look to the sacraments. Each sacrament has a mate-

91

rial element: visible, physical elements like bread, wine, oil, or human actions you can see. Each sacrament also has a form, which are the sacred words making it to be a sacred action. What is the matter in baptism? The form in baptism?"

b. "Turn to p. 82. Look at the chart describing the matter and form of each sacrament. Let us see if we can pick out which is the matter and which is the form." Direct students to pick out the matter and form and to reply in class.

7. Write on the board:

   M + F + Minister = Sacrament.

   "Every sacrament needs matter, a form, and a minister. The minister is like the sculptor in our first example of the statue of Mary. Even if we have the materials of plaster and the form of Mary, we need a sculptor to put it together. Similarly, even if we have ingredients, we need a baker to put them together to make a cake. Likewise, we need a minister to put the materials and form of the sacraments together."

8. Identify the sacraments.

   a. "Turn to p. 80. There you see Van der Weyden's picture *The Seven Sacraments*. Find each of the seven sacraments and describe how Van der Weyden has portrayed them."

   b. Write on the board: Mt 28:19; Acts 8:15–17; Lk 22:19, Jn 20:22–23; James 5:14–15; Eph 5:22–23; 2 Tim 1:16. "I have written on the board for you different scripture references. Let us see who can figure out first which reference go with which sacrament."

   c. "What is sacramental grace? Who can find the definition in our chapter?" (located on p. 83) "Read quietly the description of the sacramen-

tal graces on pp. 82–83. Now describe what graces we receive from each sacrament."

Lesson Plan for a One-day Presentation

1. Pray the Act of Love on p. 168 in the text. "We have just prayed an Act of Love. How do we get the strength to love God above all things, and our neighbors as ourselves? Through the sacraments we receive the strength to forgive injuries and really love God and others."

2. See activities 1–8, above.

3. Assign pp. 30–31 in the Activity Book.

Suggested Schedule for a Five-day Presentation

1. The meaning of sacraments
   Aim: to explain the meaning of sacraments, etymology, scriptural roots.
   Activities: see activities 1 and 2.

2. The meaning of signs
   Aim: to explain the notion of "sign" in human living.
   Activities: see activity 2; optional activity, show the filmstrip "Signs and Symbols".

3. The sacraments as signs of Christ
   Aim: to identify the sacraments as "signs of Christ".
   Activities: see activity 3.

4. Matter and form
   Aim: to explain the meaning of matter and form in general and then to apply this meaning to the sacraments.
   Activities: see activities 6 and 7.

5. Sacramental grace
   Aim: to explain the meaning of sacramental grace and to exemplify the different sacramental graces.
   Activities: see activity 8.

CHAPTER 17

God Calls Us
To Reconciliation

Background Reading for the Teacher:

Lawler, pp. 447–449, 454–461.
Hardon, pp. 506–511.

Aims:

To explain the notion of reconciliation; to identify baptism as God's call to reconciliation; to identify the scriptural roots of baptism; to identify the matter, form, and minister of baptism; to explain the effects of baptism; and to explain the baptism of desire and the baptism of blood.

Materials Needed:

Pen, paper, blackboard, text, Bibles.

Activities

1. Discuss the meaning of reconciliation.
   a. *Prodigal Son.* "Open your Bibles to Lk 15:11–32. Let us read this story together. Who does the father symbolize?" (God the Father) "The son who squandered all his money?" (us) "What is the point of the story?" (God's keen desire to forgive us and have us enter his family again)
   b. Read from the Bible on "reconciliation". Direct students to look up and read the following passages: 2 Cor 5:17–21; Col 1:15–20; Is 57:18–19; Rom 5:6–11. Guide the students in a discussion about the meaning of reconciliation from these scriptural references.
   c. Direct students to read the left column on p. 85 and then look at the detail from Giovanni di Paolo's piece *Expulsion from Paradise* on p. 86. Ask students what they think of this interpretation. Explain the symbolism.

2. Present chalk talk A, on God's call to reconciliation.

3. Direct students to read pp. 85–86, "Jesus Gave Us Baptism". Then ask, "Give me three examples from the Bible in which baptism was mentioned." Direct students to look up and read aloud the following: Mt 3:13–17 (baptism of Christ); Jn 3:1–21; 5:1–18; Lk 12:50; Mt 28:14; Acts 8:19–40. After each reference, direct a discussion on the meaning of baptism.

4. *The sacrament of baptism.* "What is the matter of baptism? Why? What is the form of baptism? Why? Who is the minister? Why?"

   Effects of baptism. "Who can find out in your text the meaning of baptismal seal? What is it? Another name for the seal is 'character'. St. Augustine gave us this name, taking it from the mark by which soliders were identified as belonging to a particular commander. To which commander do we belong?" To find the scriptural roots on the baptismal seal direct students in a discussion of the following references: Rev 7:3; Eph 1:13; 2 Cor 1:21–22; Eph 4:30. Remind students of the permanence of the seal or character.

   Have chalk talk B on "cleansing of sin" (another effect).

5. *Temples of the Holy Spirit.* Remind the students that they are temples of the Holy Spirit. Ask them to describe beautiful churches. Tell them these churches are nothing by comparison with the inner beauty of their soul in the state of grace. Direct students to read pp. 86–87, "The Effects of Baptism". Ask them to list effects of baptism. Explain each effect, and remind students that they should know these effects for a test.

2. Explain how baptism gives us the ability just to pray an Act of Faith.

3. See activities 1–6, above.

4. Assign p. 32 in the Activity Book.

Suggested Schedule for a Five-day Presentation

1. The meaning of reconciliation
   Aim: to explain the meaning of reconciliation and to compare this meaning with God's desire for reconciliation.
   Activities: see activities 1 and 2.

2. God's call to reconciliation; scriptural roots of baptism
   Aim: to continue the explanation of God's call to reconciliation and to reflect upon the scriptural roots of the sacrament of baptism.
   Activities: see activity 3.

3. Matter, form, and minister and effects of baptism
   Aim: to identify the matter, form, and minister of baptism; to explain the effects of the sacrament of baptism.
   Activities: see activities 4 and 5.

4. Baptism of desire and of blood
   Aim: to identify the two other kinds.
   Activities: see activity 6.

5. Review
   Aim: to summarize the previous lessons.
   Activities: Play a review game or use other methods for a review.

6. Direct students to read p. 87, "Baptism of Desire and of Blood", explaining that baptism of desire and blood come through the graces of the Church.

Lesson Plan for a One-day Presentation

1. Pray the Act of Faith on p. 167.

CHAPTER 18

The Rite of Baptism

Background Reading for the Teacher:

Lawler, pp. 449–461.
Hardon, pp. 511–513.

Aims:

To explain water as a sign for baptism; to explain the parts of the rite of baptism; to explain the baptismal vow; and to role play a baptism.

Materials Needed:

Pen, paper, blackboard, Bibles, texts.

Activities

1. "What words come to your mind when I say 'water'?" (Write down their answers on the board.) "What are some purposes of water?" (Write down their answers on the board.)

   "If we look at all your answers, we see three chief functions: giving life, destroying life, and cleansing. Why, then, do you think the Church uses water in the sacrament of baptism? Open your books to p. 90. Read the section 'The Use of Water'. Find examples of destroying, giving life, and cleansing. What kind of water is used in baptism? Why? What words does the priest say as he pours water on the forehead? Why?"

   "Open your Bibles to Jn 5:1–18." Explain the meaning of water in this passage.

2. Outline on the blackboard the rite of baptism for infants.
   a. Bringing the infant to the church and being welcomed at the church entrance by the priest.
   b. Liturgy of the Word
   c. Litany of the Saints
   d. Exorcism
   e. Actual baptism with water, preceded by anointing with the oil of catechumens and by renouncing Satan
   f. Final ceremonial actions: anointing with chrism, the clothing, and the lighting of the baptismal candle

3. "Why is your baptismal day your 'birthday'?"

4. Discuss the meaning of godparents. "If you had a newborn baby brother or sister, whom would you like for its godparents? Why? Give solid reasons for your choice. Listen to this description: 'The godparent chosen . . . should be a mature person (ordinarily at least sixteen years of age), a Catholic living the faith, one who is able and willing to fulfill a role of spiritual concern for the one baptized.' " (Lawler, p. 453)

5. On poster paper, sketch the symbols in the baptismal rite.

6. "What is a vow? For example, what is meant by a marriage vow? What kind of vow do we take at baptism? How do we keep our vows we made at baptism? See p. 92 for answers."

7. "Some of the early writers of the Church, such as St. John Chrysostom, described the beauty of the newly baptized, their glow and radiance, coming from their baptismal innocence. As you know, a newly baptized person is ready for heaven. Describe a newly baptized person, pointing to details of your imaginary baptized friend. Remember, spiritual beauty shines forth upon the physical."

8. Role play a baptism. "In order to make sure you know how to baptize, let us role play a baptism. Remember, in an emergency, anyone can baptize another."

Lesson Plan for a One-day Presentation

1. Pray the Creed on p. 167. Remind the students that we professed our faith at our baptism and must constantly renew it.

2. See activities 1–8.

3. Assign p. 33 in the Activity Book.

Suggested Schedule for a Five-day Presentation

1. Water, sign for baptism
   Aim: to identify and explain the significance of water in baptism.
   Activities: see activity 1.

2. Rite of baptism
   Aim: to identify and explain the different parts in the Liturgy of Baptism for infants.
   Activities: see activity 2.

3. Rite of baptism, continued
   Aim: see day 2.
   Activities: see activities 3, 4, and 5.

4. Baptismal commitment; role playing baptism
   Aim: to discuss the importance of the baptismal vow and the means to keep the vow; to role play a baptism.
   Activities: see activities 6, 7, and 8.

5. Review day
   Aim: to review the sections on baptism by a test.
   Activities: oral or written test.

CHAPTER 19

The Sacrament of Confirmation

Background Reading for the Teacher:

Lawler, pp. 462–469.
Hardon, pp. 513–520.

Aims:

To explain Christ's promise of the coming of the Holy Spirit; to see how the promise is fulfilled; to understand what happens at confirmation; to discuss the effects of confirmation and to explain the mission given at confirmation; and to review the rite of confirmation.

Materials Needed:

Pen, paper, blackboard, texts, Bibles.

Activities

1. a. "Give a description of a death scene. Pretend someone very close to you is dying. He says, 'Don't worry. I will send someone who is just like me, someone to take my place and to remind you of me.' Would this not be a consolation? This, in a way, is what Jesus did for us. How?"

    b. Read on p. 94 how Jesus promised us that he would be with us.

    c. "Read together from the Scriptures about Jesus' promise in Jn 14:25–26 and Acts 1:1–8." Lead a discussion about these references.

    d. " 'Paraclete' is from the Greek, which means 'someone who helps and guides others'. In fact, paraclete is another word for 'lawyer'. How is the image of a lawyer related to the Holy Spirit?" (The Holy Spirit speaks for us, just as a lawyer speaks for us in difficult cases.) "Remember, though, the word is paraclete, not parakeet!" (Note: psychologists tell us that associating a new word with a humorous connotation or

Chalk Talk

The Seal of Confirmation

Gives us the power to fight opposition from within (fear, evil desires, bad thoughts)

Gives us the power to fight opposition from within (bad companions, temptations)

homonym is very helpful in memorizing.)

2. a. "What kind of setting was prepared for the Holy Spirit? When we invite guests or wait for them to arrive, we clean the house and have everything in order for the guests. What did the apostles do to prepare for the Holy Spirit?" (they waited in prayer with Mary) "Is this 'setting' an example for us? How?"

   b. "Read aloud the description of the fulfillment on p. 94, under the section 'The Promise Fulfilled'. What are the symbols of the Holy Spirit?" (fire, wind) "Why are these fitting?"

   c. Have students make a collage or poster on "Symbols of the Holy Spirit".

3. Discuss related Scripture quotes: Acts 8:14–19; 11:15–17; 15:7–9; 19:1–7.

4. Discuss matter and form of confirmation by using this diagram

Matter	*+ Form*	*= Sacrament*
Laying on of hands	Words: "Be sealed with the Holy Spirit"	A mature adult in Christ
Anointing with chrism		A soldier of Jesus Christ

5. Review the notion of "sacramental seal" (see lesson plan 18). In a chalk talk discuss the seal of confirmation.

6. a. "Think of situations in which you can be a strong witness, such as: going to Mass when no one else goes or even

when people make fun of you; not listening to dirty jokes or changing the subject when friends start to tell dirty jokes; standing up for the Church and the Pope when others make fun of the Church and the Pope."

b. "Look for ways to lead others to talk about living a more Christlike life. Make up a list."

7. Use the following diagram and discuss it with the students.

Natural Life	Supernatural Life
Birth	Baptism
Maturity	Confirmation

8. "Read quietly the section entitled 'The Rite of Confirmation' on p. 96. Where does this beautiful sacrament usually take place? What happens during the actual administration of confirmation?"

Write this outline on the board. Explain each part of the rite.
a. Reading of Gospel
b. Presentation of the candidates
c. Giving of homily
d. Promise to renounce sin and Satan
e. Profession of faith
f. Imposition of hands
g. Anointing, signing with the Cross
h. Prayer: Be sealed with the Holy Spirit
i. Continuation of Mass; special blessing to the newly confirmed

9. Make up a play on a "Confirmation". Appoint a bishop, his assistants, the confirmandi. For dramatic effect, get flasks of water to symbolize the oil, a hat to represent the bishop's mitre, a cane to symbolize the staff. In your play, direct your "bishop" to ask the candidates questions. This would be a good chance for review. Suggest he ask questions about topics you have studied.

10. Have Bible readings concerning the rite of confirmation: anointing with oil (1 Sam 9:16; Ex 40:13–15; 1 Kings 19; Jn 1:41); signing with Cross (Gal 6:14); imposition of hands (Mk 10:13–16; and Mk 1:40–42).

Lesson Plan for a One-day Presentation

1. Pray an Act of Faith on p. 167.

2. See activities 1–10, above.

3. Assign p. 35–36 in the Activity Book.

Suggested Schedule for a Five-day Presentation

1. Christ's promise of the Holy Spirit's coming
   Aim: to explain Christ's promise and to lead the students to a deeper appreciation of it.
   Activities: see activity 1.

2. The fulfillment of the promise
   Aim: to see how this promise of Christ is fulfilled.
   Activities: see activity 2.

3. Sacrament of confirmation
   Aim: to identify the matter, form, minister, and effect of confirmation.
   Activities: see activities 3, 4, and 5.

4. Christian witness
   Aim: to discuss the effects of confirmation and the important mission assigned to each person confirmed.
   Activities: see activities 6 and 7.

5. The rite of confirmation
   Aim: to go over each part in the rite of confirmation.
   Activities: see activities 8, 9, and 10.

CHAPTER 20

The Gifts of the Holy Spirit

Background Reading for the Teacher:

Lawler, pp. 158–161.
Hardon, pp. 200–205.

Aims:

To explain and to appreciate the indwelling presence of God; to define the gifts of the Holy Spirit in general; to explain and exemplify each of the gifts of the Holy Spirit; to explain and exemplify the fruits of the Holy Spirit; and to summarize the teachings on the gifts and fruits of the Holy Spirit.

Materials Needed:

Pen, paper, blackboard, text.

Activities

1. Introduce the gifts of the Holy Spirit.
   a. "Read together the left-hand column on p. 99. What will happen to those who love Jesus and obey his commands? What is meant by 'the indwelling of the Trinity'? Who often mentions this mystery of God within us?"
   b. Give the students some helps for remembering God's presence: "Aspirations throughout the day tell God how much you love him; try to be quiet for a little while and remember that God is within you. While you are at work or play, ask for God's help, especially in doing what is right."
   c. "We have gifts of the Holy Spirit, received at our confirmation, or we will have developed these gifts when we receive confirmation. What are the gifts of the Holy Spirit? There is an answer on p. 99: the same spiritual powers that were poured out upon Jesus as he began his mission of preaching the Good News of salvation. The gifts make the soul alert to God's inner voice, that indwelling we were speaking about earlier. They are 'lubricants of the soul'. Why? What do lubricants do? What do the gifts do?"

2. "On the lower half of p. 99 and the top half of p. 100, read quietly the description of each of the gifts."

3. On the chalk board write a definition and example and then ask the students for their own examples:

4. "Finish reading the section on the gifts of the Holy Spirit on p. 100. What are spiritual exercises that help us keep these gifts alive?"

5. "When we think about the fruits of the Holy Spirit, we have a description of the perfect Christian. Most of us have some idea of what perfect physical beauty is and what we like to see visibly in others. The fruits give us a picture of the spiritual beauty of a healthy soul."

Look up Gal 5:22–23. Direct your students to write a description of what the perfect Christian is like, being sure to mention examples of the fruits of the Holy Spirit.

Gift	Definition	Example
WISDOM	Seeing what is truly valuable in life and judging according to God's standards	Missing a T.V. show to go to a novena or missing a party to help a sick friend
UNDERSTANDING	Insight into the faith	Understanding mysteries to some degree, in contrast to people who, in lacking this gift, do not understand them at all
KNOWLEDGE	Spiritual know-how—knowing the spiritual value and use of created things	Knowing your faith and what things are useful for heaven and what things prevent us from going to heaven (for example, knowing that watching 5 hours of T.V. every night prevents me from making a better use of my time)
COUNSEL	Seeing what is best for others in relationship to God	Giving the right advice to someone
FORTITUDE	Strength for God	Courage to give up wealth, friends, and family for Christ; giving up your life for Christ (martyrdom is the climax of fortitude)
PIETY	Affection for God as our Father who loves us and who is worthy of worship	St. Thérèse often spoke of her heavenly Father and placed so much trust in his mercy (she is famous for her gift of piety)
FEAR OF THE LORD	Fearing the judgment of and having a healthy respect for Almighty God	A movement within us which stops us from sinning, out of healthy fear

6. Make a diagram giving definitions and examples for each of the fruits. Write some of these on the board and ask your students to think of their own examples. Write their examples on the board also.

Fruit	Definition	Example
CHARITY	Constant, generous self-forgetfulness and concern for God and others	Rarely talking about themselves or feeling sorry for themselves because of their great concern for God and others
JOY	Cheerfulness in the Lord and in his gifts to us	Always trying to make others happy by their own cheerfulness
PEACE	Reflection of trust in God	Rarely worrying, always trusting in the Lord and his Mother
PATIENCE	Bearing with others' faults	Never expressing irritation and always excusing the faults of others, unless there is a duty to correct
KINDNESS	Being tender-hearted and sensitive to the needs of others	Being thoughtful about "little things"; always being there when there is some need
GOODNESS	Love that just flows out to others	Being someone who can be depended upon to do the right thing
CONTINENCE	Self-control	Knowing when to stop and say no to pleasure
MILDNESS	Being ever gentle with others	Being aware of the feelings of others; not being contradictory to others
FIDELITY	Being dependable	Never speaking behind someone's back
LONG-SUFFERING	Putting up with suffering in imitation of Jesus	Never complaining when sick
MODESTY	Holy reverence toward others and themselves	Holding themselves with dignity, not trying to "show off"
CHASTITY	Self-control about sexual desires	Being faithful to one's husband/wife, saying "no" to X-rated movies, immoral suggestions, etc.

7. "Choose one virtue or gift and describe it in detail." Ask:
   a. "Why do you want to develop it?"
   b. "How will you develop it?"

8. Tell your students stories about some of God's heroes—the saints and holy persons of the present—and how they witness(ed) to the gifts and fruits of the Holy Spirit. Some examples are St. Catherine of Siena, especially her gift of counsel; Mother Teresa of Calcutta, especially her fruit of charity; St. Francis of Assisi, especially his fruit of mildness; and St. Thomas Aquinas, especially his gifts of wisdom and knowledge. Have each of your students research a saint and tell what gift or fruit is exemplified.

Lesson Plan for a One-day Presentation

1. Pray the Act of Hope on p. 168. Remind your students that all gifts come from God because of his infinite goodness.

2. See activities 1–8, above.

3. Assign p. 37 in the Activity Book.

Suggested Schedule for a Five-day Presentation

1. The indwelling presence of God; introduction to the gifts of the Holy Spirit
   Aim: to deepen appreciation for the indwelling presence of God; to explain the importance and the meaning of the gifts of the Holy Spirit.
   Activities: see activities 1–2.

2. The gifts of the Holy Spirit
   Aim: to understand each of the gifts by definition and exemplification.
   Activities: see activities 3 and 4.

3. Fruits of the Holy Spirit
   Aim: to define and exemplify each of the fruits of the Holy Spirit.
   Activities: see activities 5 and 6.

4. Using the gifts
   Aim: to see how we use the gifts of the Holy Spirit in our lives and to identify the fruits in people's lives.
   Activities: see activities 7 and 8.

5. Review
   Aim: to strengthen each other's appreciation for the gifts and fruits of the Holy Spirit.
   Activity: test on the gifts and fruits of the Holy Spirit to make sure students have memorized the gifts and basically understand the indwelling presence of God and the fruits of the Holy Spirit.

CHAPTER 21

The Sacrament of The Holy Eucharist

Background Reading for the Teacher:

Lawler, pp. 409–429.
Hardon, pp. 457–465.

Aims:

To describe Jesus' foreshadowing and promise of the Eucharist; to describe Jesus' fulfillment of his promise of the Eucharist; to identify reasons for the signs of bread and wine; to discuss transubstantiation and Real Presence as dogmas of faith; to identify related terms; to point to the effects of the Holy Eucharist and to foster love and devotion for the Real Presence; to discuss commonly asked questions regarding the Eucharist.

Materials Needed:

Pen, paper, texts.

Activities

1. "Reading from the left column on p. 102, what was Jesus' reaction when he saw those five thousand people hungry? What happened?"

    Have students read Jn 6:1–15 and then act out a play about the reading. Appoint Jesus, Philip, and Andrew. Let the rest of the class be the hungry people, for props use a basket, some loaves of bread and drawings of the fish.

    Also ask for a narrator, who will sum up the central theme of this true event.

2. *Judas and the Eucharist.* "It was this statement of our Lord that caused many of his disciples to leave him." (Jn 6:64–71, where Judas was identified as one who would betray him) "There is a link between our faith in the Real Presence of Christ in the Eucharist, our devotion to him, and our salvation. Let us be sure we are close to him in the Eucharist."

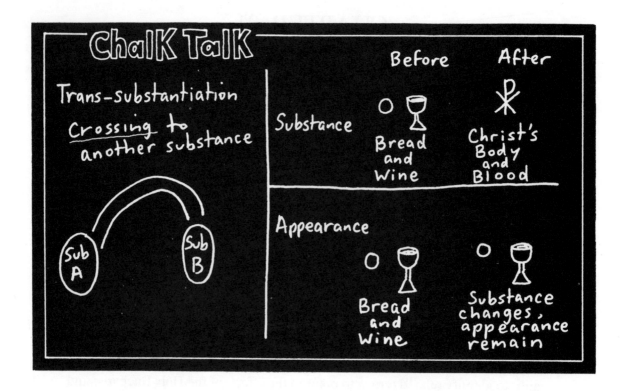

3. Have students read p. 103. Ask:
   a. "What was happening?"
   b. "What does Eucharist mean?"

4. "What are some other names for the Eucharist?" Look up other passages in Scripture related to the reference from Matthew, which is in your books: Mk 14:22–24; Lk 22:19–20; 1 Cor 11:23–24.

5. As an art project, have students make up posters showing the various titles for the Eucharist: Lord's Supper, Blessed Sacrament, Sacrament of the Altar, Bread of Life, Holy Communion, and Holy Sacrifice of the Mass. Show pictures or symbols to go with these titles.

6. "Read the section entitled 'The Sign of the Sacrament' on p. 104. Why are bread and wine used in the Eucharist? How many of you have seen pictures of starving children? What do they look like? As terrible as physical starvation is, it is not as bad as spiritual starvation. In fact, physical starvation is an ugly sign of what happens to us when we are without the Eucharist."

7. Give a chalk talk on transubstantiation.

8. Explain that there are two miracles in transubstantiation. "Miracle one is the change from bread and wine into the Body and Blood of Christ; miracle two is the appearance of bread and wine remaining, even though the change has taken place (like looking at an image of yourself in a pond and, as you go away, someone else notices your image is still there!)."

9. *Real Presence.* "What is meant by the term 'Real Presence'? Jesus is present, body, blood, soul, and divinity in the

Blessed Sacrament. Just think . . . you see me up here, looking at you? In the same way, when you enter a Catholic Church, Jesus in the tabernacle is looking at you. What a wonderful reality: let us be sure to be aware of Jesus' Real Presence."

10. "Read the section 'The Effects of the Holy Eucharist' on p. 105. Make a list of all the effects you discover. Afterward, list the effects on the board."

11. "Write a prayer to Jesus, thanking him for all the benefits he gives us in Holy Communion."

12. "Discuss what happens if you receive Communion with a mortal sin on your soul. Why?"

13. Use the following diagram and discuss the matter and form of the Eucharist.

Matter	+ Form	= Sacrament
Bread and Wine	Words: "This is my Body . . ."	Eucharist

14. Go over these important questions from pp. 105–108 with your students: Q. 129, on the exact formulation of the *de fide* dogma; Q. 134; Q. 135, which might not be clear to the students: the same Jesus who was on earth and is in heaven is present in the Blessed Sacrament; Q. 145 (Remind your students that Jesus is present in each part of the Eucharist. This is why we have patens, to catch the tiniest fragment of the host.).

Lesson Plan for a One-day Presentation

1. Pray the Act of Faith on p. 167.

2. See activities 1–14, above.

3. Assign pp. 38–39 in the Activity Book.

Suggested Schedule for a Five-day Presentation

1. Foreshadowing and promise of the Eucharist
   Aim: to describe and to appreciate more deeply Jesus' foreshadowing and promise of the Eucharist; to identify the scriptural roots of the doctrine on the Eucharist.
   Activities: see activities 1 and 2.

2. The institution of the Eucharist; fulfillment of Christ's promise
   Aim: to describe the Last Supper and to identify the institution of the Eucharist.
   Activities: see activities 3, 4, and 5.

3. The signs of bread and wine; the doctrine of transubstantiation
   Aim: to explain the significance of bread and wine as signs of the Eucharist; to define and explain the dogma of transubstantiation and also of the Real Presence; to understand the necessity of reverence before the Blessed Sacrament; to identify other terms associated with transubstantiation.
   Activities: see activities 6, 7, 8, and 9.

4. The effects of the Holy Eucharist; commonly asked questions about the Eucharist
   Aim: to point to the effects of receiving the Eucharist; to foster devotion to the Blessed Sacrament; to discuss common questions regarding the Eucharist.
   Activities: see activities 10, 11, and 12.

5. Review day
   Aim: to review various topics covered this week.
   Activities: see activities 13 and 14.

CHAPTER 22

The Eucharistic Sacrifice

Background Reading for the Teacher:

Lawler, pp. 394, 416–419.
Hardon, pp. 165–171.

Aims:

To review the Eucharist as a holy meal; to see how Mass is a renewal of Calvary; to realize how Mass is the perfect sacrifice; to explain the fourfold purpose of every Mass; to foster love for the Mass.

Materials Needed:

Pen, paper, notebook, text.

Activities

1. *Mass as a holy meal.* "The main purpose of a meal is nourishment. We cannot live without food. When was the last time you had a very happy meal? Was it in some way special? Most likely, you shared your meal with special people in your lives: family or friends; your meal itself was excellent; and, above all, you felt the warmth, intimacy, and the joy of being with loved ones. To share a meal with someone often means sharing a friendship. Frequently, when your mother or father invites guests to your home, it is a sign that your parents approve and welcome these guests as special people in their lives. This custom of sharing a meal to symbolize friendship was even more pronounced in the days of Jesus. How does this relate to the Last Supper? To the Mass?"

2. "Mass is a holy meal because the food is Christ himself. Christ then lives in each of us and together we become one body, united in charity. Mass is also a renewal of Calvary. Pretend that you have your own time machine, a machine that can take you forward or backward into time. The Mass is like such a machine. Why? The Mass renews, on our very church altars, the sacrifice of Jesus on Calvary." Give a chalk talk on the eternal Now.

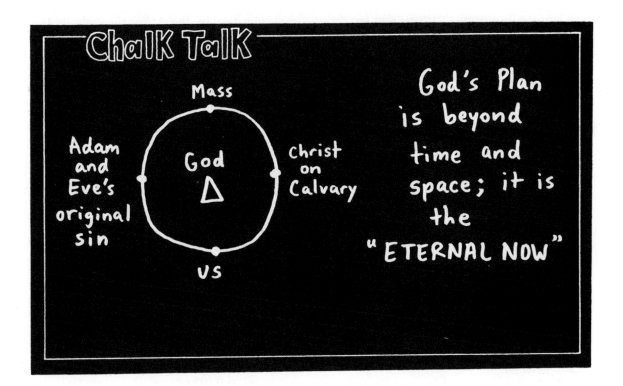

3. Read the following Scripture references on the Mass: Heb 13:8; Malachi 1:11; 1 Cor 11:26.

4. Have students read pp. 109–110 to find out: (1) how the Mass is just like the sacrifice of Calvary, and (2) how the Mass is different from the sacrifice of Calvary. As students give the answers, write them on the board. (Write on the board HOW THE MASS IS LIKE CALVARY—HOW THE MASS IS DIFFERENT FROM CALVARY.)

5. Review the meaning of "sacrifice." "We have already covered the meaning of sacrifice. What is meant by a true sacrifice? In what way is the Mass a perfect sacrifice?" (answer is on p. 109) "Look at the picture on p. 109, *The Descent from the Cross* by Rembrandt. How does this scene relate to the Mass?

Write down prayerful reflections about this picture."

6. "Turn to p. 112, Q. 152. According to this question, what are four purposes of the Mass?" Explain the four purposes, reminding the students that the most important purpose is adoration, that it is most necessary to tell God "thank you" and "I'm sorry", and that we must ask in order to receive. Give examples.

7. Turn to p. 111. Explain to your students each of the four points on "Preparing for Mass". Try to have the students frequently look at the scriptural readings for the next Mass. Ask them to write down (1) summaries, and (2) how these readings urge them to love God and others more. "Why should you arrive at church early?" (to prepare for some-

thing so important) "When you get to Church, what should you do?" (pray)

8. "Why should you spend a few minutes in prayer after Communion? Write a prayer of thanksgiving after receiving our Lord."

9. Suggest the following to your students for them to practice:
   a. "Whenever you enter a church, genuflect reverently, not quickly, thinking of the reason you are making the genuflection: to show reverence to Christ present in the Blessed Sacrament."
   b. "In church, try to kneel with your hands folded. If you sit, make sure you are praying. Don't let yourself look around and forget that the main Person you should be paying attention to is Jesus Christ."
   c. "Ask Mary to help you pay attention at Mass."
   d. "During Mass, think of the words the priest is saying and to which you are responding. Try really to mean what you say and try to join with the priest in what he says."
   e. "During the Consecration, offer Christ to the Father and offer everything in your life with Christ."
   f. "Before Communion, ask the Holy Spirit and Mary to help you receive Christ well."
   g. "After Communion, make sure you are paying attention to Christ, who, as you know, is truly present within you."

Lesson Plan for a One-day Presentation

1. Pray the Morning Offering on p. 167. Remind your students that you have just united yourselves with "the Holy

Sacrifice of the Mass throughout the world." Ask them what they think this means.

2. See activities 1–9, above.

3. Assign p. 40 in the Activity Book.

Suggested Schedule for a Five-day Presentation

1. Mass as a holy meal; Mass as a renewal of Calvary
   Aim: to review the Mass as a holy meal; to see how the Mass is a renewal of Calvary.
   Activities: see activities 1, 2, 3, and 4.

2. Mass as sacrifice; the fourfold purpose of the Mass
   Aim: to identify the Mass as the most perfect sacrifice; to explain the fourfold purpose.
   Activities: see activities 1, 2, 3, and 4.

3. Preparation for Mass; ways to increase devotion to the Mass
   Aim: to know and to practice true preparation and devotion for the Mass.
   Activities: see activities 7, 8, and 9.

4. Class Mass
   Aim: to organize a class Mass.
   Activities: The entire lesson should be spent on organization, so that the Mass will be most fittingly offered. Have the class contribute money for a stipend. Explain to them the justice of offering this monetary contribution to the priest. Ask the class for an intention close to their hearts: the recovery of someone they all know who has been sick; the end to abortion; world peace; the intentions of the Holy Father.

5. Offering of the class Mass

CHAPTER 23

The Eucharist in Our Lives

Background Reading for the Teacher:

Lawler, pp. 419–421, 428–456.
Hardon, pp. 479–481.

Aims:

To recognize the Holy Eucharist as the source and center of Christian living; to understand the Eucharist as the greatest of sacraments; to know how to receive the Eucharist properly; to prepare well; to explain various devotions to the Blessed Sacrament and their importance; and to foster a true love for Jesus in the Blessed Sacrament.

Materials Needed:

Pen, paper, notebook.

Activities

1. Tell students the story of the father of St. Thérèse. "St. Thérèse had a very holy father, Monsieur Martin, whose cause is now up for canonization. He would often be seen kneeling for a long time in church. When his friends asked, 'Why are you kneeling so long?' Monsieur Martin would reply . . . (What do you think he said?) His reply was, 'I BELIEVE.' This story leads us to today's lesson: the importance of the Eucharist in our lives."

2. In the chalk talk, discuss the Eucharist as the source and center of our faith.

3. Have the students make up posters, collages, etc. on the topic of the Eucharist, source and center of our faith.

4. "Read on p. 114 the section entitled 'Receiving the Eucharist Properly'. Then list the necessary conditions for receiving the Eucharist and be prepared to explain each condition. Can you add anything to what the book stated? For example, what do you suggest that you do to help you keep your mind on Christ when you are about to receive him? A very good way to receive Christ in Communion is to ask Mary to help you. She wants you to make a holy reception of her Son, so

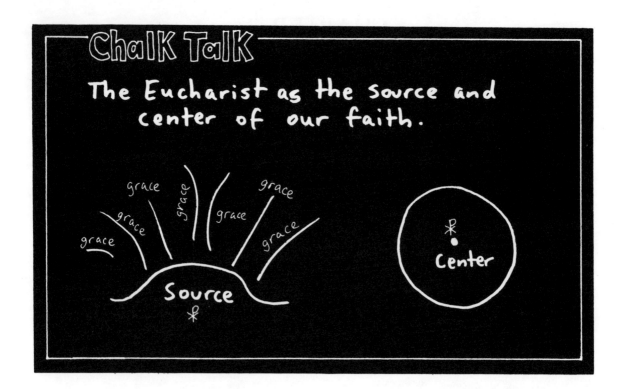

Chalk Talk

The Eucharist as the source and center of our faith.

grace grace grace grace grace grace grace

Source

Center

ask her to keep your mind on the mystery. Ask her to help you afterward to thank God for this greatest of all gifts."

5. "Why are the consecrated hosts placed in the tabernacle after Mass? There are four reasons given to you on p. 114. Jesus waits in the tabernacle for us to come to him. He is truly our best friend, and he wants us to talk to him, to pour out to him our problems, to share with him our joys, to ask him for his help. He will change our lives if we come to him as our friend. So often he is ignored in this sacrament of love. A talk with Jesus in the Blessed Sacrament is called a 'visit'. Write a prayer to Jesus in the Blessed Sacrament."

6. "Look at the picture on p. 114. What do you see? This is a picture of a monstrance. Monstrance comes from a Latin word meaning 'to show'. The

monstrance shows our Blessed Lord. The priest uses it at Benediction, which is a special prayer service during which the priest holds up the monstrance and blesses the people. How many of you have ever attended Benediction?"

7. Arrange for Benediction for your class. Make sure your students have gone through the liturgical rite in their missalettes. Pick out songs ahead of time and practice with your students. Remind them when to stand and when to kneel. Ask the priest to give a special homily for your students on devotion to the Blessed Sacrament.

8. *Other eucharistic devotions.* Tell your students about other eucharistic devotions, such as perpetual adoration. Investigate whether there are any churches in your diocese promoting perpetual adoration. Also see if you

have any monasteries or religious houses devoted to perpetual adoration. Another devotion you can explain is the Forty Hours Devotion. Relate to your students the story of St. John Neumann and the Forty Hours Devotion.

9. Tell students the story of how St. Clare of Assisi started a group of nuns devoted to prayer. These nuns are called today the "Poor Clares". St. Clare was of course very devoted to the Eucharist. "One day some wild Saracens attacked the village where Clare and her Sisters lived. St. Clare went out to meet them holding the monstrance." (What is a monstrance?) "What do you think happened?" (They went away. Jesus' power in the Eucharist overcame their fierce attack.) "What is the lesson we can learn from this true story?"

Lesson Plan for a One-day Presentation

1. Pray "O Sacrament Most Holy, O Sacrament Divine; all praise and all thanksgiving be every moment Thine."

2. See activities 1–6, above.

3. Assign pp. 41–42 in the Activity Book.

Suggested Schedule for a Five-day Presentation

1. The Eucharist: greatest of sacraments.
   Aim: to understand the greatness of the Eucharist.
   Activities: see activity 1.

2. The Eucharist, source and center of Christian living
   Aim: to recognize the Eucharist as the source and center of Christian living.
   Activities: see activities 2 and 3.

3. How to receive the Eucharist properly; ways to prepare for the Eucharist
   Aim: to know the Church's requirements for a worthy Communion; to identify ways to foster a greater reverence and love in receiving Communion.
   Activities: see activity 4.

4. Devotions to the Blessed Sacrament
   Aim: to identify and to explain various devotions to the Blessed Sacrament; to exemplify models of eucharistic devotion by relating the lives of some of the saints; to practice eucharistic devotion with correct liturgical rubrics.
   Activities: see activities 5, 6, 7, 8, and 9.

5. Paraliturgy
   Aim: to practice what has been learned about eucharistic devotion by participating in a prayer service honoring the Eucharist.
   Activities: participating in the Benediction already arranged; making a visit. It would be helpful to show the students the monstrance, luna, and other sacred vessels you have taught them about.

CHAPTER 24

Sin and Mankind

Background Reading for the Teacher:

Lawler, pp. 291–299.
Hardon, pp. 183–185, 435–437.

Aims:

To review the doctrine on original sin; to define temptation and to identify its kinds; to be aware of personal temptations and to fight them; to identify, define, and exemplify the seven capital sins; to define occasions of sin and to resolve to avoid them at all costs; to define sin and to identify the kinds of sins; to regard mortal sin as worse then physical death; to resolve to commit no sin; to point out the three conditions for mortal sin and to explain these conditions; to define venial sin and to see it as a most serious evil; and to identify and to explain the development of a Catholic conscience.

Materials Needed:

Pen, paper, text.

Activities

1. Review original sin and the loss of sanctifying grace in chalk talk A.

   "Look at the picture on p. 117. What do you see?" (Adam and Eve being expelled from paradise) "Quietly write down how you think Adam felt, and how Eve felt as they were being banished from paradise. In a few minutes, we will hear what you have to say."

2. Write TEMPTATION on the board. Write the Latin root *temptatio,* "testing". "How is a temptation a 'testing'? Look up the definition on p. 118. What does your text say a temptation is?" Write the definition on the board. Explain other parts of the discussion on p. 118, "The False Promises of Temptation".

3. In chalk talk B discuss the meaning of occasions of sin.

115

4. Use the following diagram to discuss sin.

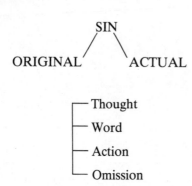

5. Discuss the meaning of mortal sin. "What is meant by 'mortal'? 'Mortal' comes from a Latin word, *mors,* which means 'death'. Why is mortal used as an adjective for these kinds of sins?" (These sins are deadly sins, killing the life of grace in the soul.) "Act out a murder." (Have a play gun.) Direct the murdered victim to lie passively on the classroom floor. "What would you do if he were really murdered? Would you just sit and stare? Of course not? Yet, this is what we seem to do in regard to that which is far more terrible: death of souls. Some examples of death—mortal sin—are a deadly wound; a dead body; separation from a lifeline of a deep-sea diver, of an astronaut, of a patient on a respirator; story of St. Louis' mother, Blanche, who told him as a young boy she would rather see him dead than that he should ever commit a mortal sin. Did Blanche love Louis? Are you able to say this—I would rather see you dead than that you should ever commit a mortal sin—to your family and friends? To yourself?"

6. Explain and exemplify the three conditions for committing a mortal sin. This is an extremely important lesson, so make sure you repeat and answer all possible questions. Test your students on their knowledge of the three conditions. Give an example for condition 3 (freely choosing). Direct student A to take Student B's hand and place a play gun in it. Direct student A to have student B's hand point to student C and pull the trigger. Have student C fall down, as if he were dead. Ask the class, "Did student B have a free choice in this matter?"

7. Discuss venial sins. "Right now think of someone whom you greatly respect and would never wish to offend. It could be a mother, grandmother, special teacher, or special friend. Now, what would you think if I said, 'It is all right to slap _____, just don't kill her/him.' " (Let students express their reflections.) "How does this relate to venial sins?" (No sin, no matter how "venial", is a light thing, for it offends One who so tenderly loves us, One to whom we owe so much respect and love.)

Discuss Cardinal Newman's reflection with the students. "Cardinal Newman, a great cardinal of the nineteenth century, said it is worse that one venial sin be committed, than that many terrible disasters occur around the world. Why? Is he right? Why is he right?"

Compare venial sin to a tear. "If you have a tear in your blouse or shirt, what should you do? If you did not mend it, what would happen?" (the tear would get so large that the blouse or shirt would be ruined.) "How is this tear like venial sin?" (If we do not stop committing venial sins, we shall soon start committing mortal ones.)

8. Have the students list the seven capital sins, being sure they understand why

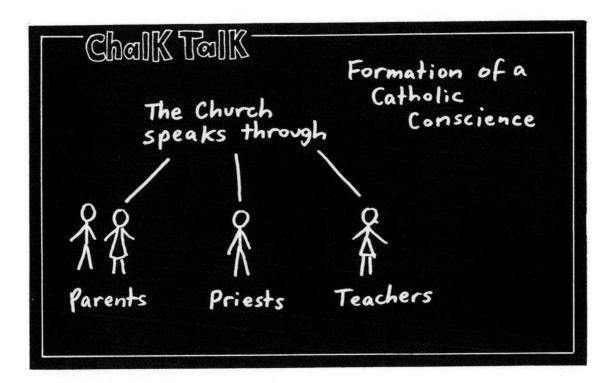

they are referred to as capital or deadly sins.

9. In chalk talk C discuss the formula for a correct conscience.

10. Give a review quiz. Write:
    a. T for thought, W for word, A for action, or O for omission
    b. P for pride, Gr for greed, L for lust, A for anger, Gl for gluttony, E for envy, or S for sloth

    a. (*T-L*) George often has impure thoughts, which he freely chooses to dwell upon.
    b. (*A-Gl*) Bill comes home after school and eats five pieces of cake because it tastes good. He feels a little sick, but he keeps taking more.
    c. (*O-Gr*) Susie chooses to miss Sunday Mass so she can work more hours.
    Money comes before all else with Susie, even though she is not poor.
    d. (*W-E*) Jean spreads ugly rumors about Mary, who was elected to be head cheerleader for the seventh-grade sports team. Jean wanted to be the head cheerleader.
    e. (*W-A*) Joe "blew up" at Tom when Tom refused to help Joe cheat on his homework.
    f. (*O-S*) Jane rarely hands in her homework when it is due. She spends hours before the T.V. set each night.

Lesson Plan for a One-day Presentation

1. Say the Act of Contrition on p. 167.

2. See activities 1–9 above.

3. Assign pp. 43–44 in the Activity Book.

Suggested Schedule for a Five-day Presentation

1. Review of original sin; temptation: definition, kinds, ways to fight
   Aim: to review doctrine on original sin and to show man's fallen condition and propensity to sin; to identify, explain and exemplify the meaning of temptation and occasion of sin.
   Activities: see activities 1, 2, and 3.

2. Sin: kinds of sin, gravity of mortal sin
   Aim: to define sin and to identify and explain the kinds of sin; to identify the seven capital sins; to regard mortal sin as the worst tragedy that could befall one; to resolve to commit no sin.
   Activities: see activities 4, 5, 6, and 8.

3. Three conditions for mortal sin
   Aim: to review yesterday's lesson; to explain thoroughly the three conditions for mortal sin.
   Activities: see activities 5 and 6.

4. Venial sin: its nature and its evil
   Aim: to explain the nature of venial sin and to differentiate it from mortal sin; to regard venial sin as worse than the most repulsive and deadly disease.
   Activities: see activity 7.

5. Formation of a correct conscience
   Aim: review.
   Activities: see activities 9 and 10.

Notes:

CHAPTER 25

God's Mercy and Forgiveness

Background Reading for the Teacher:

Lawler, pp. 96, 125–136.
Hardon, pp. 181–185, 433–437.
Mt 11:25–30.
Lk 17:11–19; 18:1–14; 19:1–10; 15:11–32.
Jn 21:15–19.

Aims:

To see through Scripture God's revelation of himself as a merciful God; to distinguish between hatred for the sin and love for the sinner; to understand the meaning of "change of heart"; to identify means to grow in this change of heart; to resolve to love God and others more; to see and to accept Christ's call to carry the Cross; to identify practical penances; and to define sorrow and to explain the two kinds of sorrow: contrition and attrition.

Materials Needed:

Pen, paper, blackboard, text, Bible.

Activities

1. "Some people think of God as a merciless judge, ready to pounce on them the moment they sin. Scripture tells us otherwise. God is all-just, but he is also all-merciful. Turn to p. 121 and begin reading the first column."

   "God is all-just and all-merciful. We must include both truths in our thoughts about God. To ignore either one is an error." Discuss this in chalk talk A.

2. Have Bible readings on God's mercy: Lk 15:11–32; 17:11–19; Jonah 4; Lk 19:41; 13:34; Ps 34; 103; 145; 1 Jn 4. Conduct a discussion on these readings or have the students compose meditations or draw pictures about the scriptural themes.

3. Give examples of Jesus' great love for sinners (see p. 121). Have students read Lk 19:1–10 and then perform a play about it. Appoint a boy to be Zacchaeus; perhaps a ladder could serve as

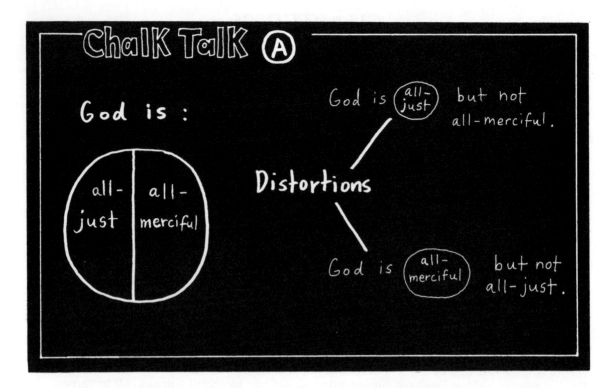

Chalk Talk Ⓐ

God is:

all-just | all-merciful

Distortions

God is (all-just) but not all-merciful.

God is (all-merciful) but not all-just.

a tree. Have the narrator conclude the skit by pointing to the lesson: Jesus loves the *repentant* sinner. "Does Jesus' love for sinners mean he approves of their sins? Why or why not? How can you hate the sin but love the sinner? Read p. 121, under the section 'God Loves the Sinner but Hates the Sin'." Act out Jn 8:1–11. (You may want to change the sin of adultery to a more common sin among your seventh-graders: cheating, lying, gossiping, etc.)

4. Have chalk talk B on "change of heart".

   Put up outline on board:

   I.   Change of heart (define).
   II. Means to growing in a change of heart
        a. Examination of conscience
        b. Remembering your death and judgment
        c. Going to monthly confession

   Lead a discussion on these points taken from pp. 121–123 in the text.

5. Direct your students to read the examination of conscience found on p. 171. Direct your students to "make up your own examination of conscience. Think of yourself, your weaknesses and strong points. What do you have to work on?"

6. *Death and judgment.* Tell true stories about young people who have died (death does not respect age). Ask your students: "What does it mean to die? Are you ready to die? Should you be ready to die?" Tell them the story of what a priest once said to a worldly man: "Repeat and mean what you say, 'I will die, I will be judged, and I will go to hell . . . and I don't care.'" The

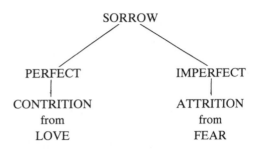

"St. John Vianney was a very holy priest who spent hours in the confessional. Many times he would say to his penitents, 'I weep because . . .' " Ask your students to fill in what they thought he would say. Compare their answers to what St. John answered: "I weep because you do not weep."

9. Discuss the relation of the Passion of Christ to sin. Relate the truth that sin caused Christ to suffer. Point to a crucifix as you explain.

Lesson Plan for a One-day Presentation

1. Begin with recitation of Ps 51. (You can select the most fitting parts.) Explain that this psalm is a plea for God's mercy, the theme of the lesson today.

2. See activities 1–9, above.

3. Assign pp. 45–46 in the Activity Book.

Suggested Schedule for a Five-day Presentation

1. God's revelation as mercy
   Aim: to eliminate distortions of God and to stress his mercy to sinners who recognize their sinfulness.
   Activities: see activities 1 and 2.

worldly man was converted by just thinking of what he was saying.

7. Make up a poster on the theme of "Take up your cross and follow me." Give examples of daily acts of penance: not complaining; obeying immediately, giving in to someone else's wishes, not saying bad things about someone who talks behind your back, giving up some T.V. Ask your students to give you examples of "good penances for seventh-graders". Suggest they make up a bulletin board or large poster on the penances listed.

8. Use a diagram to discuss sorrow.

2. Hatred for the sin, love for the sinner
   Aim: to distinguish carefully between hatred for the sin and love for the sinner.
   Activities: see activity 3.

3. "Change of heart"
   Aim: to examine the meaning of the importance of a "change of heart"; to state precise and practical ways to grow in a true change of heart; to resolve to love God and neighbor sincerely.

Activities: see activities 4–5.

4. "Change of heart" and "carrying your cross"
   Aim: see day 3; to identify ways to follow Jesus in carrying our daily cross.
   Activities: see activities 6 and 7.

5. Sorrow
   Aim: to define sorrow and to distinguish between contrition and attrition.
   Activities: see activities 8 and 9.

Notes:

CHAPTER 26

The Sacrament of Penance

Background Reading for the Teacher:

Lawler, pp. 470–485.
Hardon, pp. 481–500.

Aims:

To identify and to explain the scriptural roots of confession; to state the chief elements making up the sacrament of Penance; to point to the signs and the effects of the sacrament of Penance; to grow in prayerful appreciation and love for the sacrament; to express the five steps of good confession; to describe the rite of reconciliation and to understand the meaning of the ceremonies, symbols, and words; and to go over important questions that arise about the sacrament of Penance.

Materials Needed:

Pen, paper, blackboard, text.

Activities

1. Review original sin and actual sin; have students read p. 126, first paragraph.

2. Compare the sacrament of Penance to a daily bath or shower: we need to clean ourselves frequently, not only physically but spiritually. Compare the growth of disease among unclean people to the growth of sin among people who do not bathe often in the sacrament of confession.

3. Have students read next the two paragraphs on p. 126. Optional: Direct students to act out: appoint Jesus and ten disciples (Recall: Thomas wasn't there and neither was Judas.)

4. Use the chalk talk.

5. *"Peace be with you."* "Peace is something everyone seems to want. How do people feel during wartime? They want one thing. What is it?" (peace) "Why?

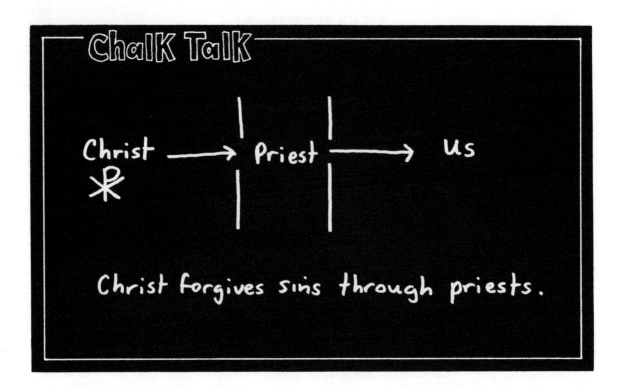

Christ → Priest → Us

Christ forgives sins through priests.

Have you ever felt really worried and upset? For example, you were the one who set off the fire alarm; your principal calls you into his office. How do you feel? Many, many people are flocking to psychologists and psychiatrists today. Why? They want 'peace of mind'. Why?"

6. "If you forgive men's sins they are forgiven; if you hold them bound, they are held bound." "What great power a priest has! Why does he have this power? It is not really his power, but it is _____ power." (God's) "When we go to confession, we are really confessing our sins to Jesus Christ, represented by the priest."

7. Prepare a chart on matter and form.

Matter	+ Form	= Sacrament
Confession of Sins	Words of Absolution	Forgiveness of Sins

Put this outline on the board. Explain each point.

Effects of the sacrament of Penance
I. Taking away our sins
II. Restoring the life of grace to our souls
III. Taking away the punishment we deserve
   More sorrow — More punishment taken away
IV. Giving us all the actual graces we need to do good and avoid sin in the future

124

8. Have students read the section "How to Make a Good Confession" on p. 128. Explain each of the steps, stressing:
   - The need, even before examining your conscience (point 1), of praying to the Holy Spirit for light and guidance.
   - The need to make an unhurried, thorough examination of conscience.
   - The meaning of true sorrow. (See lesson plan for Chapter 25.)
   - The need for firm resolution. "To say to God, 'I'm sorry', but then say, 'But I'm going to do it again', is like saying to your friend, after pinning him on the floor and hitting him very hard, 'I'm sorry', and then proceeding to give him a few more slugs and punches. Would your friend really think you are truly sorry? Compare this situation with your saying to God, 'I'm sorry, but I'll do it again'."
   - The importance of doing your penance right after going to confession: "Chances are you could forget to do it later."

   Use mnemonics to help students remember the five steps to a good confession (see p. 128): ESRCP (Each sinner receives Christ's pardon).

9. Go over the rite of Penance, explained on pp. 128–129.

10. Ask a priest to come into your class and give a talk on the sacrament of Penance, encouraging the students to frequent the sacrament, reminding them of the seal of confession, explaining the rite. (If you are a priest, you can use your priestly gift to help your students.)

11. Tell the students the story of St. John Vianney, "who used to hear three hundred to four hundred confessions a day, spending sixteen hours night and day in the confessional. St. John had a special gift of reading souls, and people would come from all over France for the consolation of going to such a holy priest for confession. Often St. John would assign a penance of going into the church where he had statues of Christ at his scourging and Christ after his Crucifixion. He directed his penitents, including young men, to kiss these statues in reparation for their offense to Christ. Why is this a good penance?" Or tell the story of Damian the Leper Priest, "who would have to quite literally 'shout out' his sins to his confessor because Damian was in a rowboat alongside the ship. His confessor could not come near him, because of his leprosy, so Damian humbled himself to shout his sins outside. Why did he do this?"

12. Ask a priest to conduct a special "rite of reconciliation", often found in missalettes and designed especially for groups. If possible, take your students to a church. Remind them to say "thank you" to the priest for the gift of absolution.

Lesson Plan for a One-day Presentation

1. Pray the Memorare on p. 170. "We stand before Mary, sinful and sorrowful, asking her help to make a good confession and to understand this sacrament."

2. See activities 1–12, above.

3. Assign pp. 47–48 in the Activity Book.

Suggested Schedule for a Five-day Presentation

1. The scriptural roots of reconciliation.
   Aim: to identify and to explain the scriptural basis for the sacrament.
   Activities: see activities 1, 2, 3, 4, and 5.

2. Chief elements making up the sacrament of Penance and effects of the sacrament

   Aim: to explain the chief elements; to identify and to appreciate the effects.

   Activities: see activity 7.

3. Five steps of a good confession; the rite of Penance

   Aim: to go over the five steps of a good confession and to grow in a prayerful response to the sacrament as described in the rite.

   Activities: see activity 8.

4. Explanation of the rite of Penance

   Aim: to describe the rite of Penance and to understand the meaning of the ceremonies, symbols, and words.

   Activities: see activities 9, 10, and 11.

5. Receiving the sacrament of Penance

   Aim: to provide the setting for individual confessions by participating in a penitential service, including the Liturgy of the Word, an examination of conscience for seventh-graders, individual confessions, and communal acts of sorrow and gratitude.

   Activities: see activity 12.

Notes:

CHAPTER 27

The Sacrament of Anointing

Background Reading for the Teacher:

Lawler, pp. 485–493.
Hardon, pp. 540–547.

Aims:

To describe Jesus' great love for the sick and the suffering; to identify and to explain the scriptural roots of the Anointing of the Sick; to state the purpose of the sacrament and to describe its history; to identify and to explain the signs and effects of the sacrament; to describe the rite and to familiarize oneself with it; and to define and to explain the role of indulgences.

Materials Needed:

Pen, paper, notebook, blackboard, crucifix, two candles, small bowl of water, match.

Activities

1. Use a diagram to explain:

    the effects of original sin . . .

    PAIN   ILLNESS   DEATH

    . . . on the Human Race

2. Discuss the purpose of suffering. Read in the Scriptures: Rom 8:17; 2 Tim 2: 8–13.

3. Use a diagram to explain: on the sacrament of Anointing.

ANOINTING

Gives spiritual aid to enable us to use our pain for our holiness

Heals us if it is God's will

Prepares us for death

4. "Turn to p. 135. What do you see? This is a famous picture by Fra Angelico, *Raising of Lazarus.* Describe the expressions." Have students read the section "Jesus Shares His Healing Power" on p. 133. Point out the scriptural basis for this sacrament. Discuss bodily cures. Remind your students that this sacrament possesses the power, if God so wills, to heal physically as well as spiritually.

5. Write ANOINTING FOR GLORY on the board. "This is the name St. Thomas Aquinas gives to this sacrament. Why?" Have students read "The Purpose of This Sacrament" on p. 134. "What was the strange attitude among some Catholics regarding this sacrament? Why? How did the Church correct this attitude?"

6. Ask the class, "What would you say to someone who regarded the Anointing of the Sick as a sure sign of death?" Discuss the students' answers.

7. Prepare a chart on matter and form.

Matter	+ Form	= Sacrament
Anointing with blessed oil	Prayer	Anointing of the Sick

8. Have a student research Greek athletes' use of oil and report to the class. How does this help our understanding of the sacrament?

9. Have the students list the effects of this sacrament.

10. Have students read "The Rite of Anointing" on pp. 134–135. "Where can the administration of this sacrament take place? Describe in detail what goes on during an Anointing of the Sick."

Direct the students to role play an Anointing of the Sick. Appoint a priest, a family, and a sick person. Prepare a small table with a crucifix, two candles, and a glass of water. Direct the student "priest" to sprinkle holy water and to give a short sermon on the meaning and purpose of the sacrament. (You may wish to write this out for him.) See the *Rites of the Catholic Church* (which your pastor should have) for further directions.

11. Look up programs for shut-ins in your parish. Direct your students to interview someone in their parish or family who has received the Anointing of the Sick. Explain that the word *Viaticum* comes from the Latin for "traveling companion". "Why is this Eucharist called a 'traveling companion'?"

12. Explain differences in indulgences. See pp. 136–137 in the text.

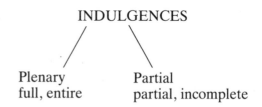

INDULGENCES

Plenary
full, entire

Partial
partial, incomplete

13. Tell stories of saints and holy people who dedicated themselves to the sick, such as St. John of God, Rose Hawthorne, Mother Mary Potter (foundress of the Little Company of Mary), and Mother Teresa of Calcutta.

14. Ask a priest to come into your class to give a talk on his experiences with the sacrament of the Anointing of the Sick. Ask him to include any examples of people who have been physically cured.

15. Teach your students a prayer for a holy death. Remind students that the most important moment in their lives is their death. Urge them to pray often for a happy and holy death. Suggest their praying not only to our Lady ("Pray for us now and at the *hour of our death*") but also to St. Joseph, who is the patron of a happy and holy death.

Lesson Plan for a One-day Presentation

1. Pray the Hail Mary and also say "Mary, Consolation of the Dying, pray for us." Remind the students that they have just asked our Lady to help them now and at the hour of their deaths.

2. See activities 1–14, above.

3. Assign pp. 49–50 in the Activity Book.

Suggested Schedule for a Five-day Presentation

1. Jesus' love for the sick and suffering
   Aim: to describe and to appreciate the great compassion of our Lord for the sick, suffering, and dying.
   Activities: see activities 1, 2, and 3.

2. Scriptural roots of the Anointing of the Sick; purpose and history of the sacrament
   Aim: to point to the scriptural roots of this sacrament; to explain the purpose and history of the Anointing of the Sick; to have a healthy attitude toward it.
   Activities: see activities 4, 5, and 6.

3. Signs and effects of the sacrament
   Aim: to identify the signs and to explain the effects.
   Activities: see activities 7, 8, and 9.

4. The rite of Anointing; the meaning and purpose of indulgences
   Aim: to describe the actual rite; to be familiar with it; to appreciate the symbolism; to act correctly during the rite; to define and explain indulgences.
   Activities: see activities 10, 11, and 12.

5. Review day/or experiences of a priest
   Aim: to review by means of a test or to listen to the personal experiences of a priest who has given the sacrament often.
   Activities: see activities 13, 14, and 15.

Notes:

CHAPTER 28

The Sacrament
Of Holy Orders

Background Reading for the Teacher:

Lawler, pp. 429–446.
Hardon, pp. 520–531.

Aims:

To present an overview of the three main divisions of the sacraments: initiation, healing, and service; to cite and to explain references on the institution of the priesthood and on apostolic succession; to distinguish between the common priesthood and the ordained priesthood; to identify and to explain the hierarchies in the priesthood; to point to the signs and effects of the priesthood; to extol the dignity of the priesthood; to foster a true respect and love for the priest; and to promote priestly vocations.

Materials Needed:

Pen, paper, blackboard, text, Bible.

Activities

1. Give chalk talk A on the division among the sacraments.

2. "When you think of Christ, what comes to your mind? What is Christ like?" (Describe Christ to your students after they have responded.) "Because Christ loves us so much, he leaves us with visible representatives in whom and through whom Christ himself speaks and acts.

Who are they?" Write on board: SACERDOS, ALTER CHRISTUS. "This is a Latin expression meaning that a priest is 'another Christ'."

3. Have students read pp. 139–140, "Jesus Gives Us the Sacrament of Holy Orders". When did Jesus institute the priesthood? Along with being ordained to the priesthood, to what other office were the apostles ordained at this time?" (They were ordained to the

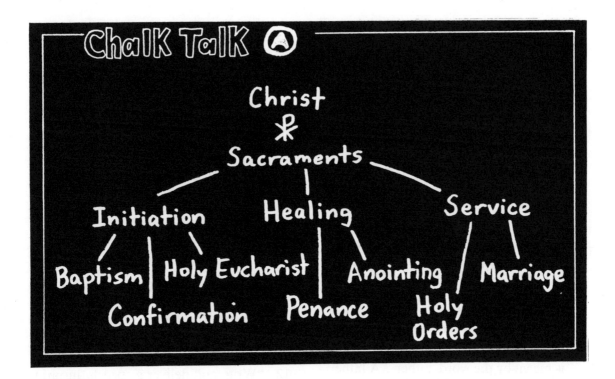

Chalk Talk Ⓐ

Christ
☧
Sacraments

Initiation   Healing   Service

Baptism | Holy Eucharist | Anointing / Marriage

Confirmation   Penance   Holy Orders

office of bishop.) "What is meant by apostolic succession? Did the apostles know at the time that there would be apostolic succession? Cite a source to support your answer." (cf. p. 140)

4. "In addition to Lk 22:19, you should memorize Jn 20:21–23. Look up this passage now. Why should you know this passage? How does it relate to the priesthood?" (It relates to the priesthood because Jesus gave the apostles the power to forgive sins, something only a priest can do.)

5. Have students read "A Royal Nation of Priests" on p. 140. "What is meant by the 'common priesthood'? How are you and I priests? How does one become an ordained priest?" (through a call from God) Discuss.

6. Explain the word "vocation" is from the Latin *vocare,* 'to call', and that a priestly vocation is a call from God. Make sure the students understand that everyone has a vocation and that the priesthood is just one kind of vocation. Point out the picture on p. 139, Duccio's *The Calling of the Apostles Peter and Andrew,* which shows this call. "Describe what you see in the picture." It is important in this section to clarify the precise role of women in the Church and the truth that they are not called by God to become priests. Be ready to answer questions intelligently. Read in the Scripture about the call to the priesthood: Heb 7:24–25; Jn 14:6; 1 Tim 2:5; Heb 10:11–15.

7. On the chalkboard draw a diagram of the hierarchies in the priesthood, and discuss it with the students.

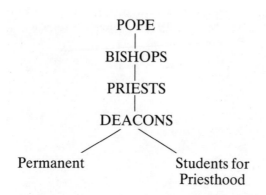

POPE
|
BISHOPS
|
PRIESTS
|
DEACONS

Permanent   Students for
                   Priesthood

Have students read the section "The Levels in Holy Orders" on pp. 140–141. "In your notebook, write three headings: bishop, priest, and deacon. Under each heading, write the duties corresponding to each office."

8. "Why is a priest called 'Father'? What is meant by the word 'father'? A father is one who begets life. How does a priest bring new life into the world?" (He brings spiritual life.) "Look up 1 Cor 4:15" ("It was I who begot you in Christ Jesus").

9. Prepare a chart on matter and form.

Matter	+ Form	= Sacrament
Laying on hands	Prayer	Holy Orders

10. "Look at the picture on p. 141. What is happening? Why is the bishop placing his hands over the young man?" Make copies of "rite or ordination" for your students. (Write to the diocesan vocation director.) After going over the parts and explaining the symbolism, direct your students to act out an ordina-tion. Be sure to have a chair in the center of the room for the bishop, a miter, crozier, and other episcopal apparel (made up, of course); a piece of cloth for a stole; if it is an ordination to the priesthood, a pillow for a prostration of the young man being ordained, etc.

11. "What is a priest to you?" Give the students time to think or write their descriptions. Let them say aloud their responses to the question. "St. Thérèse, expressed beautifully the vocation of a priest: 'With what love, O Jesus, I would carry you in my hands when, at my voice, you would come down from heaven. And with what love would I give you to souls!' Just think: Christ comes to you personally, to me, through the hands of priests. Write some reflections and prayers of gratitude for the gift of priests."

12. "Write and deliver a speech, inspiring someone to respond to Christ's call to the priesthood. Pretend the person is hesitant and fearful." "Write to a seminary and ask for information on the priesthood." Invite a priest and/or a deacon to come into your class and speak on vocations.

Lesson Plan for a One-day Presentation

1. Pray the prayer to St. Michael, p. 170. Add "Mary, Queen of Priests, pray for us" or "St. John Vianney, Patron of Priests, pray for us."

2. See activities 1–12, above.

3. Assign pp. 51–52 in the Activity Book.

Suggested Schedule for a Five-day Presentation

1. Three sacramental divisions; institution of the priesthood

Aim: to explain the three divisions of the sacraments; to see how the priesthood is one of service; to identify the scriptural institution of the priesthood.

Activities: see activities 1, 2, 3, and 4.

2. The common priesthood and the ordained priesthood; hierarchies in the priesthood

   Aim: to distinguish between the common and the ordained priesthood and to clarify contemporary misconceptions; to explain the hierarchical division in the priesthood.

   Activities: see activities 5, 6, 7, and 8.

3. The signs and effects of the priesthood

   Aim: to identify and to explain the signs and effects of the priesthood.

   Activities: see activities 9 and 10.

4. The dignity of the priesthood

   Aim: to cultivate a deep respect and love for the priesthood and for priests; to promote priestly vocations.

   Activities: see activity 11.

5. Reinforcement

   Aim: to reinforce the previous lessons by a talk by a priest or deacon or by a test.

   Activity: see activity 12. If a priest or deacon does come to your class, be sure to prepare your students beforehand. Direct them to ask intelligent questions in advance. Suggest they take notes.

Notes:

CHAPTER 29

The Sacrament of Matrimony

Background Reading for the Teacher:

Lawler, pp. 494–508.
Hardon, pp. 356–367, 531–540.

Aims:

To identify the Old Testament roots of marriage; to state the twofold purpose of marriage; to read New Testament statements on marriage; to describe a Catholic marriage; to become familiar with the rite of Matrimony; to answer modern day attacks on marriage; and to prepare intelligently for a good Catholic marriage.

Materials Needed:

Pen, paper, blackboard, text.

Activities

1. Have students read on p. 144, first part, "It is not good for the man to be alone . . ." Discuss the need for community; the male-female complementarity, etc. Discuss the command to procreate: ("Be fruitful and multiply . . .").

2. Explain in the chalk talk that the two purposes of marriage are mutual love and procreation.

3. "How can the husband help his wife know, love, and serve God? How can the wife help her husband know, love and serve God?"

4. Have students read the section "The Sacrament of Matrimony" on p. 145. Explain that the permanence of marriage is the norm, not an ideal. Ask: "What did Jesus say about marriage? What is marriage a symbol of?"

5. Parallel a marriage between husband and wife with the marriage between God and his people to show the similarities.

Chalk Talk

Marriage =

Mutual Love

+

Procreation

6. Read in the New Testament about Matrimony: Mk 10:7–8, 8–9; Eph 5:25, 32; 1 Cor 7:7.

7. Have students read the section "What is Christian Marriage?" on p. 145. Have the students list all the conditions for a valid marriage. Ask: "What is meant by an invalid marriage?"
   Describe cases of marriage:
   • "Joan's husband, Rick, is a drunk and often comes home and beats her and the children. May Joan separate from her husband? Can she remarry, since Rick is so cruel and such a poor father?"
   • "Dave's wife, Marilyn, has been put in a psychiatric ward and might not get better. In fact, the doctors told Dave that Marilyn might have permanent mental and emotional problems, making her unfit for living at home. Dave has three little children. Can he obtain a divorce and remarry? At the time he married Marilyn, she was perfectly balanced; she developed these problems later."

Point out to the students the serious reality of the marriage vow: "through good times and bad, in riches or in poverty, in sickness or in health".

8. Have students read "The Rite of Matrimony" on pp. 145–146. Act out a marriage rite. (You may wish to check *The Rites of the Catholic Church*.) Tell the students to read through the marriage vows carefully.

9. Ask: "Why is marriage holy?" Comment on: "It takes three to make a marriage." "What are the effects of the sacrament of matrimony? Why do a husband and wife, a father and mother, need special graces from a sacrament? Make a list of temptations to impatience, self-pity, etc. that occur in married life."

10. Have students read "Modern Day Attacks on Marriage", first paragraph of section, p. 146. List all the attacks described. Counter them with the Catholic positions.

11. Tell stories of married saints, such as St. Rita, who was beaten by her husband; and St. Monica, who converted her non-Catholic husband by the beauty and power of her virtue. Another married couple, who are presently up for canonization, are Mr. and Mrs. Martin, the father and mother of St. Thérèse.

12. Discuss the absolute need for foresight and preparation. "Even though you are only in seventh grade, you should be

thinking about the importance and the difficulty of making a good choice if you marry. If your parents are very careful when buying a car or VCR or computer, how much more careful should you be when entering into a lifelong commitment. You should pray much and ask our Lady to send you the perfect spouse at the right time if marriage is God's will for you."

13. Invite as a guest speaker a priest who has witnessed marriages or a priest who works closely with married or engaged couples to speak to your class. Suggest that he tell your students of the challenges and also the dangers they will face as teens. Perhaps you could also invite a married couple, known for their joyful fidelity and dedication to the Church.

Lesson Plan for a One-day Presentation

1. Pray the Glory Be. Remind the students that everything is for the honor and glory of God. Marriage is not just for one's own satisfaction, but is for God. Pray: "Mary and Joseph, models for happily married couples, pray for us."

2. See activities 1–13, above.

3. Assign pp. 53–54 in the Activity Book.

Suggested Schedule for a Five-day Presentation

1. Old Testament roots of marriage; two-fold purpose of marriage

   Aim: to identify and to explain the roots in the Bible for the Church's teaching on marriage; to analyze the two necessary elements in every marriage.
   Activities: see activities 1, 2, and 3.

2. New Testament statements on marriage; the meaning of a Catholic marriage

   Aim: to identify precise New Testament references on marriage; to compare the marriage between man and woman to the Covenant between God and his people; to describe the conditions necessary for a valid marriage.
   Activities: see activities 4, 5, 6, and 7.

3. The rite of Matrimony

   Aim: to become familiar with the rite of Matrimony; to appreciate its meaning and beauty.
   Activities: see activities 8 and 9.

4. Modern day attacks on marriage; practical recommendations for preparing for marriage; the holiness of marriage

   Aim: to identify and to refute contemporary attacks on the sacredness of marriage; to prepare practically for marriage; to appreciate the sanctity of marriage.
   Activities: see activities 10, 11, and 12..

5. Reinforcement
   Aim: to reinforce topics taught.
   Activities: see activity 13.

CHAPTER 30

Mary, Mediatrix of Grace

Background Reading for the Teacher:

Lawler, pp. 97–111.
Hardon, pp. 150–171.
St. Louis de Monfort, *True Devotion to the Blessed Virgin.*

Aims:

To identify love for Mary as the mark of a true Christian; to describe Mary's role as Jesus' Mother and ours; to point out Mary's privileges; and to explain the meaning of a total consecration to Mary and to foster authentic devotion to Mary.

Materials Needed:

Pen, paper, blackboard, texts.

Activities

1. Write AD JESUM PER MARIAM on the board.

   Explain that we go to Jesus through Mary.

2. Relate how important mothers are. Explain how we cannot imagine how much Mary meant to Jesus. His last act before he died was to give Mary to us as our Mother. (See p. 148.)

3. Have students read the section "Mary's Role in Our Salvation" on pp. 148–149. Have them list all the events in Mary's life that mark her role in our salvation. After a few minutes, direct some of the students to write parts of their lists on the board.

4. "Mary is the first and perfect disciple of Jesus. On poster paper, make three columns: 'Mary's Example', 'Theme', 'Me'. List detailed examples of Mary's practice of Christian virtue; explain your example and put this explanation under the heading 'theme'. Then show how you, in a very practical way, can imitate Mary."

Example:

Mary's Example	Theme	Me
Mary remained near Jesus during the Passion.	Being faithful to the Lord when suffering comes.	I must remain faithful to Christ even when it means being rejected by my friends.

"You can draw or cut out pictures to enhance or to help explain your thoughts."

5. "Make a booklet entitled, 'Life of Mary'. Pictures and prayers as well as your own reflections can be put in this booklet."

6. Discuss Mary's privileges. "Mary's privileges are the jewels, the beautiful clothes with which God adorned his Mother, our Queen. What are these privileges? See p. 149, right column."

7. Give chalk talk A.

8. Give chalk talk B on Mary, mediatrix of grace.

9. "What is the easiest way to become a saint? The saints tell us devotion to Mary, especially a total consecration to Mary, is the easiest way. Why? Research the life of a saint and find evidence of his or her devotion to Mary."

10. Tell stories of deathbed conversions, miracles of grace, even physical mira-

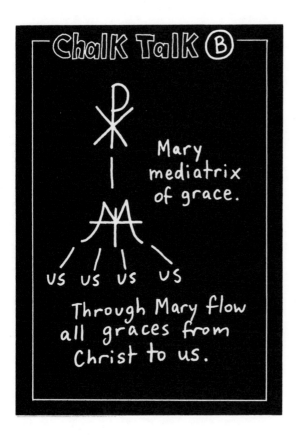

Chalk Talk Ⓑ

Mary mediatrix of grace.

US US US US

Through Mary flow all graces from Christ to us.

a. Mary loves you: "She loves them more tenderly, more tenderly than all the mothers in the world together. Take the love of all the mothers of the world for their children. Pour all that love into the heart of one mother for an only child. . . . Yet Mary's love for each of her children has more tenderness than the love of that mother for her child."

b. Mary provides for all your needs: "She provides them with everything they need for body and soul."

c. Mary leads and guides you: "Follow her and you cannot go wrong", says St. Bernard.

d. Mary intercedes for you: "She appeases him with her prayers, brings her servants into closest union with him, and maintains that union."

12. Talk about Marian apparitions. Tell the stories of Our Lady of Guadalupe, of the Miraculous Medal, of Lourdes, of Fatima, of La Salette. Show filmstrips correlating with your stories. A few recommendations: Our Lady of La Salette, Our Lady of Lourdes, Our Lady of Guadalupe, Our Lady of Fatima.

cles wrought through Mary's intervention. Some good sources for these stories are *The Glories of Mary,* by St. Alphonsus de Liguori; *The Secret of the Rosary,* by St. Louis de Montfort; and *True Devotion to the Blessed Virgin,* by St. Louis de Montfort.

11. Explain the meaning of total consecration to Mary. Tell your students that the basic element in such a consecration is absolute trust in the motherly, loving concern of Mary for the Church and for them individually. Remind them that when they trust Mary so completely, she will most certainly care for their spiritual and temporal concerns. You may find it helpful to list the following advantages, taken from *True Devotion:*

Lesson Plan for a One-day Presentation

1. Pray the Litany of the Blessed Virgin Mary on p. 169.

2. See activities 1–12, above.

3. Assign pp. 55–56 in the Activity Book.

Suggested Schedule for a Five-day Presentation

1. The importance of love for Mary
   Aim: to inspire a love for our Lady by stressing its importance.
   Activities: see activities 1, 2, 10, and 11.

2. Mary's role in our salvation

   Aim: to identify Mary's role as Jesus' Mother and ours; to appreciate this role by deeper gratitude and affection.

   Activities: see activities 3, 4, 5, and 8.

3. Mary's privileges

   Aim: to state the doctrines concerning Mary's privileges.

   Activities: see activities 6, 7, 8, and 12.

   Special activity: The story and correlating filmstrip are very helpful for reinforcing one of the Marian doctrines. For example, showing Our Lady of Lourdes reinforces the doctrine of the Immaculate Conception.

4. True devotion to Mary; the meaning of a total consecration to Mary

   Aim: to describe the Church's teachings on devotion to Mary; to foster more authentic Marian piety.

   Activities: see activities 9, 10, and 11.

5. Marian paraliturgy

   Aim: to reinforce spiritually the week's lesson by participation in a Marian paraliturgy.

   Activities: You may choose one of the following, or think of others:

   a. A group Rosary: have various leaders selected for each decade; direct some of your students beforehand to make up fitting meditations on the mysteries of the Rosary; have the students choose a prayer intention or intentions, such as world peace, the end to abortions, the repose of the soul of someone who has died, and so on. End with the Litany of the Blessed Virgin Mary.

   b. A group consecration to Mary: you frequently find well-planned paraliturgies in some of the October or May missalettes.

Notes:

Appendix

LESSON PLAN OVERVIEW

To plan the year's course, write a title or phrase for the material you are going to cover in a week's time and the pages where the material can be found in the textbook. For example: 1. *Introduction, pp. 9–11.*

1. _____

2. _____

3. _____

4. _____

5. _____

6. _____

7. _____

8. _____

9. _____

10. _____

11. _____

12. _____

13. _____

14. _____

15. _____

16. _____

17. _____

18. _____

19. _____

20. _____

21. _____

22. _____

23. _____

24. _____

25. _____
    _____

26. _____
    _____

27. _____
    _____

28. _____
    _____

29. _____
    _____

30. _____
    _____

31. _____
    _____

32. _____
    _____

33. _____
    _____

34. _____
    _____

35. _____
    _____

36. _____
    _____

37. _____
    _____

38. _____
    _____

39. _____
    _____

40. _____
    _____

BASIC TRUTHS OF THE CHRISTIAN FAITH

1. *Who created us?*
   God created us.

2. *Who is God?*
   God is the all-perfect Being, Creator and Lord of heaven and earth.

3. *What does "all-perfect" mean?*
   "All-perfect" means that every perfection is found in God, without defect and without limit; in other words it means that he is infinite power, wisdom and goodness.

4. *What does "Creator" mean?*
   "Creator" means that God made all things out of nothing.

5. *What does "Lord" mean?*
   "Lord" means that God is the absolute master of all things.

6. *Does God have a body as we have?*
   No, God does not have a body, for he is a perfectly pure spirit.

7. *Where is God?*
   God is in heaven, on earth, and in every place: he is the unlimited Being.

8. *Has God always existed?*
   Yes, God always has been and always will be: he is the eternal Being.

9. *Does God know all things?*
   Yes, God knows all things, even our thoughts: he is all-knowing.

10. *Can God do all things?*
    God can do all that he wills to do: he is the all-powerful one.

11. *Can God do also something evil?*
    No, God cannot do evil, because he cannot will evil, for he is infinite goodness. But he tolerates evil in order to leave creatures free, and he knows how to bring good even out of evil.

12. *Does God take care of created things?*
    Yes, God takes care of created things and exercises providence over them; he preserves them in existence and directs all of them toward their own proper purposes with infinite wisdom, goodness, and justice.

13. *What purpose did God have in mind when he created us?*
    God created us to know him, to love him and to serve him in this life, and then to enjoy him in the next life, in heaven.

14. *What is heaven?*
    Heaven is the eternal enjoyment of God, who is our happiness, and the enjoyment of all other good things in him, without any evil.

15. *Who merits heaven?*
    Every good person merits heaven— that is, he who loves God, serves him faithfully and dies in his grace.

16. *What do the wicked deserve who do not serve God and who die in mortal sin?*
    The wicked who do not serve God and who die in mortal sin merit hell.

17. *What is hell?*
    Hell is the eternal suffering of the loss of God, who is our happiness. This means a deep and real personal suffering.

18. *Why does God reward the good and punish the wicked?*
God rewards the good and punishes the wicked because he is infinite justice.

19. *Is there only one God?*
There is only one God, but in three equal and distinct Persons, who are the most Holy Trinity.

20. *What are the three Persons of the Holy Trinity called?*
The three Persons of the Holy Trinity are called the Father, the Son, and the Holy Spirit.

21. *Of the three Persons of the Holy Trinity, was one "incarnate", that is, made man?*
Yes, the Second Person, God the Son, became "incarnate", that is, was made man.

22. *What is the Son of God made man called?*
The Son of God made man is called Jesus Christ.

23. *Who is Jesus Christ?*
Jesus Christ is the Second Person of the most Holy Trinity, that is, the Son of God made man.

24. *Is Jesus Christ God and man?*
Yes, Jesus Christ is true God and true man.

25. *Why did the Son of God become man?*
The Son of God became man to save us, that is, to redeem us from sin and to regain heaven for us.

26. *What did Jesus Christ do to save us?*
To save us, Jesus Christ made satisfaction for our sins by suffering and sacrificing himself on the cross, and he taught us how to live according to God's laws.

27. *What must we do to live according to God's laws?*
To live according to God's laws we must believe the truths which he has revealed and observe his commandments, with the help of his grace, which we obtain by means of the sacraments and prayer.

SACRAMENT BOOK

Direct the students to compile a "Sacrament Booklet", consisting of:

1. Definitions of each of the sacraments
2. Matter and form for each of the sacraments
3. Sacramental grace of each of the sacraments
4. Pictures (can be cut out from Catholic periodicals) or drawings of the symbols in the sacrament
5. Appreciation, reflection, or prayer in gratitude for the beauty and importance of the sacrament

This is a long-range project, so give your students enough time to work on it.

REVIEW GAMES

Review games are valuable in helping the students to remember the lesson. Students are usually more motivated to memorize things to win a game than to complete a straight memorization assignment. Games can also be used to build confidence (when the teacher gauges the questions to the ability of each student) and cooperation among the students. Often times, the reward of winning is enough for students. However, you might want to give little prizes such as holy cards or medals, etc. The games below will be marked according to the grade level at which they work best: 1° = grades 1–3; 2° = 4–6; and 3° = 7–8.

Bible Baseball 1°, 2°

1. Set up bases around the room.

2. Pick teams.

3. Ask a question of a student on one of the teams. If he gets the answer, the student goes to first base and the next student is up for a question. If he misses the answer, he is out. The next teammate must answer the same question. If three students on the same team cannot answer the question or if three questions are missed their team is out and the other team is up.

4. Points are received for "home runs", that is, when a student has gotten to all three bases and reached home base.

Tic Tac Toe 1°, 2°

1. Pick sides. "X" goes first.

2. Draw grid on the chalkboard.

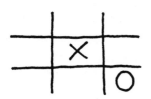

3. Ask a question of a student on the first team. If he answers it correctly, his team chooses where to put the "X". If he answers incorrectly, the other team has a chance to answer the question. If the "O" team answers correctly, they can choose where to put the "O", and then they get their turn. If they answer incorrectly, they merely get their normal turn.

4. The team that gets three "'X's", or three "O's" in a row wins the round. Losers start the next round.

Peek-a-Boo 2°, 3°

1. Pick Sides.

2. A student from one team stands at the front of the room with his back to the chalkboard.

3. The teacher writes a word on the board.

4. Teammates can give only one clue to the member at the board. The student at the board chooses which of his teammates will give the clue. A different clue-giver must be chosen for each word.

5. If the student says the word on the board, his team gets a point and the next member of the team gets a chance at the board. If he fails to say the word, the other team gets to play.

Credo 2°, 3°

(This game takes a long time.)

1. Each student plays for himself.

2. Have each student fold a piece of paper in half and cut at the fold.

3. On one half sheet of paper, draw a "CREDO" card (see illustration).

4. Write 25–30 words on the board that relate to the material that you are reviewing; have the students write fill-in-the-blank questions for each word. Assign which word(s) each student will write a question for, so that all the words have a question. Each question should be on a separate piece of paper.

5. Have the students write a word from the board into every box on their "CREDO" cards. No repeats. The middle box is a FREE space.

6. Collect the questions from the students. Mix them up and read a question aloud, twice. If the student has the word on his "CREDO" card, he draws a line through the word, but is careful not to make it unreadable, so that the teacher can check it if the student wins. Proceed as with a BINGO game.

7. When a student gets a row or black out or four corners he says, "Credo!" If all the words the student crossed out were correct, he must say the words and the questions to the class before he wins.

Modified "Hangman" 2°, 3°

1. Pick teams (2 or more).

2. Think of a message (or have a list ready beforehand). For example: GOD IS GOOD.

3. Write the spaces for the message on the chalkboard. ____/____/_____.

4. A member from the first team guesses a letter. If he is correct, the team gets a point for every time the letter occurs, for example: if he had guessed a "G" his team would get 2 points (G ___/ ___/G ____) and another member of his team gets to guess the next letter. If he is wrong, write the letter on the board as a letter already used. The turn goes to the next team.

5. If anyone on any team can guess the message before all the letters are in place, he may interrupt and give the answer. His team receives 5 bonus points. If the student guesses incorrectly, his team has 5 points taken away.

6. The team that reaches 100 (or 50, or 25, etc.) first wins. The game can also be played with a time limit instead of a point limit.

Divine Pursuit 2°, 3°

Materials: game board (see illustration), a die, takens (such as figurines of Jesus, Mary and the saints), plastic or paper chips, cards with catechism questions and answers written on them.

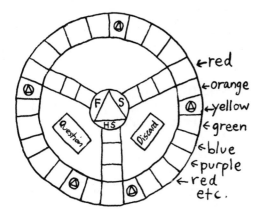

←red
←orange
←yellow
←green
←blue
←purple
←red
etc.

Note: Use six colors for the squares, using each color in succession around the circle and straight paths.

1. Each player (or team) rolls the die. The lowest roll is first. The player to the left is next, etc. Takens start at the center of the board.

2. To take a turn, roll the die and move the number of spaces indicated on the die. If the person lands on a yellow space, another player draws and asks a question. If the player cannot answer, his turn ends. The correct answer is read aloud and the card put in the discard pile. If the player answers correctly, he receives a red chip and his turn ends. If the player lands on a square of any other color, his turn is over.

3. When a player has obtained three chips, he moves to the center, which must be reached by an exact roll. The player must then answer a question from the pile. If he answers correctly, he has won the game. If not, the player must leave the center on the next turn, and return for another question.

4. When no more questions are left in the question pile, shuffle the discard pile and it will become the question pile again.

149

DRAMATIZATION

Dramatization of a scene from Scripture, or the Rosary, etc., helps the students to use all their faculties and senses in learning. For the younger children, you might have to write and produce the play yourself, but older children (grades 3–8) can make and produce the play themselves. Thus, the students use their imagination and creativity as well as their senses. Below are three ways you can dramatize a scene.

**Popsicle Stick Puppets
and Shoe Box Theater**

The puppets are easily made from popsicle sticks and either felt, construction paper, or cut out pictures. For example:

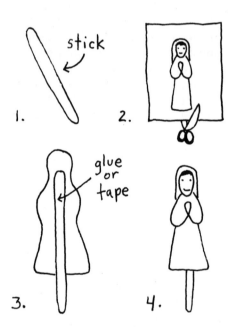

long side (the slot toward the top will be where you insert the puppets; the slot toward the bottom will be for inserting the backdrop, or scenery).

For the theater, take a large shoe box and cut two slots, one toward the top of the box on one of the long sides, and the other toward the bottom of the box on the opposite

Masks

To identify the different characters in a play without having to make elaborate costumes, it is quite easy to make masks. For example, if you wanted to dramatize the temptation and fall of man, you could make the following masks out of paper and have the students color them, or make them out of construction paper.

EVE

ADAM

GOD

SERPENT

ANGEL

Costumes do not have to be elaborate to be effective. An old sheet, bathrobe, or remnants of material are usually all you need. If you need a crown and a miter these can be made out of construction paper and sized to fit the head of the actor. For example:

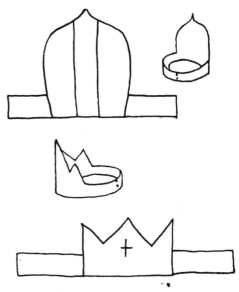

To show the change from perfect happiness to the fallen state of Adam and Eve, or the original delight of Satan at man's fall, then disappointment at God's promise, make the masks reversible. The masks may be handheld and then flipped at the proper time during the skit. For example:

Beards too are easily made of paper, then hooked around the ears:

Adam before the Fall.

Adam after the Fall

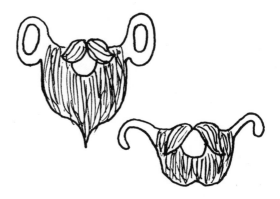

Swords can be cut out from cardboard and covered with aluminum foil, and chains can be made by linking paper strips together.

(Chains and swords might be used for a play on Joan of Arc or on Joseph being sold into slavery, etc.)

Notes:

Grade 7 Activity Book Answer Key

N.B.: Many of the questions require the student to give an answer in his own words. Where specific doctrinal or historical points that the student is expected to learn in this course of studies are looked for, suggested answers (or outlines) are provided to the teacher. In other places, the student is expected to write a response for which no specific answer is needed. A note is provided to indicate that answers will vary.

Students should answer in complete sentences.

Note: Definitions of terms are all found in the *Words to Know* section of the textbook.

Chapter 1

II.
1. We know that God exists because of the order and design of the universe.
2. We know that God must be great and powerful.
3. We know that God must be pleasing and beautiful.

III.
Circle: 1, 5   *Cross out*: 2, 4, 6
Underline: 3

Chapter 2

1. word
2. collection
3. inspiration
4. describe
5. Good News
6. Catholic
7. revealed
8. Tradition

Chapter 3

II.
1. T; 2. F; 3. F; 4. T; 5. F

Chapter 4

II.
1. T; 2. F; 3. F; 4. F; 5. T.

Chapter 5

II.
1. God first appeared to Moses in a burning bush. God told Moses to return to Egypt in order to deliver the Jews from their slavery. God also revealed his name to Moses calling himself "Yahweh" which means "I am".
2. The Israelites sprinkled the blood of the Passover lamb on the doorposts as a signal that the home would be spared from the tenth plague.
3. As the Israelites approached the Red Sea God intervened to save them from the Pharaoh's troops. God parted the mighty waters of the sea and made a clear path for the Israelites to travel through. As soon as the last of the Israelites reached the other side of the sea, the waves came crashing down upon the Egyptians.

Chapter 6

II.
Isaiah 61:1: This prophecy states that the Lord anointed him with the Spirit. Therefore, he will preach to the meek and brokenhearted; he will liberate the captives.
Isaiah 40:11: This prophecy states that the Messiah will be like a shepherd to his flock. He shall take special care of the young.
Micah 5:1: This prophecy states that the Messiah, the judge of Israel, will suffer.

Chapter 7

II.
Luke 7:13: This passage reveals that Jesus had human emotions, like compassion, just as all humans do.
John 11:5: This passage reveals again that Jesus had human emotions. This passage speaks of Jesus' love for Martha, her sister and Lazarus.
John 11:35: This passage reveals that Jesus' emotions moved him deeply. Jesus wept for Lazarus.
III.
Mark 4:35−41: This passage shows that Jesus had the power to calm the forces of nature, in this case, the wind and the sea. Jesus has control over nature.
John 2:1−11: This passage shows that Jesus had the power to change water into wine. This is the first indication that Jesus could perform miracles.
Luke 4:33−37: This passage shows that Jesus had the power to exorcise unclean spirits from their victims.

Chapter 8

II.

1. The treasure and the pearl symbolize the Kingdom of heaven.
2. This parable tells us that God's Kingdom is so great that a man would sell all his earthly possessions to buy into it.

III.

against anger: Jesus says that the fifth commandment warns the people against murder yet he warns the people against anger. He says that those who die angry at their brother shall come into judgment also.

occasions of impurity: Jesus warns the people of even looking on someone with lust because this is an instance of adultery. Jesus says that it is better to cut off the offending part than for the body to go to hell.

divorce: Jesus speaks against divorce in this passage. He says that divorce causes adultery because if the woman remarries she is guilty and whoever marries her is guilty.

on oaths: Jesus says that we should not swear at all. We should say what we mean. Anything beyond this is from the evil one.

retaliation: Jesus refutes the old law of retaliation. Instead, he institutes a new law that says not to retaliate but to bear the attack and even be open to more attack. This way you will not be guilty of retaliation.

love of enemies: Jesus says to love even your enemies and to pray for your persecutors. In this way you can develop your gift of love in order to be like God who is perfect love.

Chapter 9

1. We learn:

    1) The gift must be offered with a pure and sinless heart.

    2) The offering is a thanksgiving to God for his blessings and protection.

    3) The offering of sacrifices shows sorrow for sin and a desire for forgiveness.

2. We call Jesus our perfect High Priest because he is the greatest priest of God. Jesus was the sinless Son of God who came down from Heaven in order to give perfect worship to the Father.

3. The Resurrection of Jesus proved that Jesus' sacrifice worked! His sacrifice made up for every sin and reconciled us to the Father. The Resurrection showed that God accepted this sacrifice.

Chapter 10

II.

Grace is a supernatural gift from God given to us through Jesus Christ. God gives us this gift because he loves us. There are two kinds of grace: Sanctifying grace makes us holy and pleasing to God; it makes us his children and temples of the Holy Spirit. It also gives us the right to live in Heaven. Actual grace gives us help every day in order to do good and avoid evil. We receive sanctifying grace through the sacraments which Christ instituted when he was on earth. We receive actual graces through the guidance of the Holy Spirit whom Christ sent to man.

Chapter 11

II.

1. F; 2. T; 3. F; 4. T; 5. F;
6. F; 7. F; 8. T.

Chapter 12

II.

Jesus promised the gift of infallibility to the Church when he spoke of sending the Spirit of Truth to the Church at the Last Supper. Thus, through the Holy Spirit the gift of infallibility is given to the Pope in order to protect the message of salvation that Jesus has given to the Church.

Chapter 13

II.

1. A; 2. S; 3. S; 4. A; 5. S; 6. A.

Chapter 14

II.

1. F; 2. C; 3. H; 4. C; 5. C; 6. H; 7. F.

Chapter 15

II.

Fortitude, Temperance, Prudence, Justice.

Chapter 16

Luke 2:13−14: Glory to God in the highest, and peace to his people on earth. Lord God, heavenly King, almighty God and Father, we worship you, we give you thanks, we praise you for your glory. Lord Jesus Christ, only Son of the Father, Lord God, Lamb of God, you take away the sin of the world: have mercy on us; you are seated at the right hand of the Father, receive our prayer. For you alone are the Holy One, you alone are the Lord, you alone are the Most High, Jesus Christ, with the Holy Spirit, in the glory of God the Father. *Amen*.

Matthew 21:1−11: Holy, holy, holy, Lord, God of power and might, heaven and earth are full of your glory. Hosanna in the highest. Blessed is he who comes in the name of the Lord. Hosanna in the highest.

Luke 11:1−4: Our Father, who art in Heaven, Hallowed be thy Name. Thy Kingdom come, thy will be done on earth as it is in Heaven. Give us this day our daily bread and forgive us our trespasses as we forgive those who trespass against us. And lead us not into temptation but deliver us from evil. *Amen*.

John 1:29: Lamb of God, you take away the sins of the world: have mercy on us. Lamb of God, you take away the sins of the world: have mercy on us. Lamb of God, you take away the sins of the world: grant us peace.

Matthew 8:5−8: Lord, I am not worthy to receive you, but only say the word and I shall be healed.

Chapter 17

II.

1. The "Good News" of our salvation is that the separation of man from God due to original sin has come to an end because of Jesus our Savior. The reconciliation, or reunion, of mankind with God in loving friendship is good news to mankind because it means that God continued to love man even though he disobeyed God. God's love for man is so great that he sent his only Son to earth to reunite God and man.

2. The Baptismal Seal is an invisible mark which shows God that we have been united to Jesus by Baptism and have become his children. Baptism gives us the right to receive the other sacraments. Baptism washes away the effects of original sin from our souls. Baptism fills us with a new life of sanctifying grace.

Chapter 18

II.
Answers will vary.

IV.
Only when ordinary water is used in Baptism according to the plan of Jesus can it receive the power to free us from sin and fill us with God's life. The water must be poured over the forehead of the person to be baptized while the priest says: "I baptize you in the name of the Father, and of the Son, and of the Holy Spirit."

Chapter 19

II.

When the apostles were gathered in one **room**, suddenly a sound came from Heaven like the rush of a mighty **wind**. Tongues of **fire** appeared and came to rest on the **head** of each of them. All were **filled** with the **Holy Spirit**. They began to express themselves in **foreign** tongues.

III.

1. People expect adults to have the responsibility of spreading the faith to others. Adults are to witness or stand up for Jesus and never be ashamed to proclaim to all the world Christ crucified. (Answers may vary from this.)

2. Adult Christians must be strong in faith.
Adult Christians are filled with the Holy Spirit.
Adult Christians must be responsible.
Adult Christians must be mature.

Chapter 20

II.

Understanding   Answers will vary.
Fear of the Lord
Counsel
Wisdom
Piety
Knowledge
Fortitude

Chapter 21

II.

The Eucharist and death: Jesus said that the Old Testament fathers did not have the Eucharist. These fathers ate manna alone and they are dead. He said that if the Jews eat of the bread come down from Heaven (Eucharist), they will not die.

The Eucharist and eternal life: Jesus said to the Jews that if they eat of his Body and drink of his Blood they will gain eternal life with him.

The Eucharist and resurrection from the dead: Jesus said to the Jews that if they partake of the Eucharist, he will raise them up on the last day.

The Eucharist and the life of God: Jesus said that he who partakes of the Eucharist will live by him. Since Jesus is God, his life is by the Father, those who partake of the Eucharist shall live with God.

Chapter 22

II.

1. death; Resurrection
2. opportunity
3. victim
4. offered; Last Supper
5. Friday
6. priest
7. apostles
8. sacrifice
9. gifts; Body; Blood

Chapter 23

II.

1. Jim is practicing only the bare minimum of his faith. He sees Holy Communion as a once-a-year obligation rather than as the opportunity to become closer to Christ.

2. Even though Cathy receives Holy Communion faithfully each week, she does so with the stain of mortal sin on her soul. Cathy has been receiving Jesus Christ for these two years but she has not been receiving his life-giving grace. Therefore, Cathy should go to Confession in order to release herself from the grip of mortal sin. Then she will receive the gifts of Holy Communion.

3. Stephen should not go to Communion because he is conscious of committing a mortal sin. Stephen should make an effort to go to Confession at the first opportunity in order to be released from mortal sin and to re-establish God's life of grace to his soul.

Chapter 24

II.

1. **M**: The Third Commandment.
2. **M**: The Fourth Commandment.
3. **V**: The First Commandment.
4. **V**: Any or all of the Second, Fourth, Sixth or Eighth Commandments.
5. **V**: The Tenth Commandment.
6. **M**: The Sixth and Ninth Commandments.
7. **N**.
8. **V**: The Seventh Commandment.
9. **M**: The Fifth Commandment.
10. **M**: The Sixth and Ninth Commandments.

Chapter 25

II.

1.
   1) I am an adopted child of God and heir to Heaven.
   2) Jesus freely chose to suffer and die on the Cross for me.
   3) God has given me a special mission in life and wants me to live with him for ever.
   4) God wanted me to be born; he gave me human life.

2.
   1) Listen carefully to the Mass, especially to the Gospel.
   2) Listen to the homily given at Mass.
   3) Study my religion lesson well.
   4) Study the Gospels and Letters of the New Testament.

3.
   1) Examine my conscience for a few minutes every night.
   2) Practice little acts of penance or self-denial.
   3) Think about the four last things.
   4) Ask the Holy Spirit to help me use the gifts he has given me.

5) Receive the Holy Eucharist worthily and receive the sacrament of Penance monthly.
6) Pray to know myself better.

Chapter 26

II.
1. three
2. weaken
3. forgave
4. shared
5. Penance; confession; reconciliation
6. mortal; times
7. examination of conscience; true sorrow; promise to change; telling our sins honestly; doing the penance given
8. privately; face
9. Christ
10. ashamed; embarrassed; trust

Chapter 27

II.
1. F; 2. T; 3. F; 4. T; 5. F; 6. T.

III.
You would remind Steve about how much God loves him and wants him to be happy for ever in Heaven. Encourage him to think about the things in his life which may have separated him from God's love. He should tell God he is completely sorry for anything and everything that he has ever thought, said, done or not done which has displeased God. He should tell God he loves him above everything and thank him for his love and forgiveness.

Chapter 28

II.
1. B; 2. D; 3. P; 4. B; 5. D;
6. P; 7. B; 8. P.

Chapter 29

II.
1. Wives are to submit themselves to their husbands in everything. Wives should be subject to their husbands, just as the Church is subject to Christ. For husbands are the head of their wives, just as Jesus is the Head of the Church. Thus, wives should reverence their husbands.
2. Husbands are to love their wives just as Jesus loved the Church. Jesus gave himself for the Church, so that he might cleanse it, sanctify it to make it holy and without blemish. So men must love their wives as their own bodies. Paul says, ''He that loves his wife loves himself.''
3. Saint Paul says that a man should leave his father and mother and be joined to his wife. Then they two shall be one flesh. This mystery corresponds to the mystery of Christ's relationship to the Church.

Chapter 30

II.
1. Mary loved God above all things. Unlike Eve, Mary obeyed the will of God in every way. Mary had great faith, trust and love for God. She truly was full of grace and deserved her title, Mother of God.
2. Answers will vary.
3. Mary courageously stood near Jesus as he suffered and died on the Cross. Together with Jesus, she prayed to God to accept his death for the forgiveness of our sins.
4. After Mary ascended into Heaven, Mary stayed with the apostles as they prayed for the gift of the Holy Spirit. For the rest of her time on earth, she was a mother to the Church. She continued to teach of Jesus until she was taken into Heaven herself.